Going the Extra Mile

Insider Tips for Long-Distance Motorcycling and Endurance Rallies

RON AYRES

Whitehorse Press
North Conway, New Hampshire

Whitehorse Press books are also available at discounts in bulk quantity for sales and promotional use. For details about special sales or for a catalog of motorcycling books and videos, write to the publisher:

Whitehorse Press
P.O. Box 60
North Conway, New Hampshire 03860-0060
Phone: 603-356-6556 or 800-531-1133
E-mail: Orders@WhitehorsePress.com
Internet: www.WhitehorsePress.com

ISBN 1-884313-39-6

5   4

Printed in the United States of America

To Rose, Hope, and Ronnie, who are eagerly waiting for their legs to reach the passenger footpegs.

Acknowledgements

I'd like to acknowledge the contributions made to the development of this book by members of the long-distance motorcycling community. Although I've learned a lot by spending time in the saddle, it pales by comparison to what I've learned from my long-distance colleagues.

I want to thank Norm Grills and Bill Thweatt for help with the photographs and for reviewing the book for accuracy.

I want to thank Don Arthur, a committed long-distance rider and medical doctor. I relied on Don to help ensure that my comments about the medical aspects of riding are accurate.

I also want to thank my sister-in-law and proof editor, Roberta Robinson, and my wife Barbara Robinson for help in making the final manuscript more readable.

Thanks to Dan Kennedy and Lisa Dionne at Whitehorse Press for encouraging me to write this book. I owe a special thank you to Lisa for the hours that she dedicated to suggesting revisions that improved the quality of the book. The result would not have been nearly the same without her contributions.

Contents

Foreword

Long-distance motorcycle riding is not for everyone, but the chances are that since you've opened this book you've either caught the long-distance bug or, at the least, you have an interest in long-distance riding.

While there are thousands of visitors every month to the Iron Butt Association's Internet web page, most of them are not interested in riding in an Iron Butt event. Rather, after hearing about Iron Butt rides—which generally start at 1,000 miles in 24 hours—they want to learn the secret to riding their motorcycles farther than they do now. They would also like to do it safely and comfortably.

Many riders hope to discover how to see more of the world from their motorcycle in a limited amount of time by significantly increasing their daily mileage. Surely anyone who can ride 1,000 miles in a day, as Ron Ayres has done many times, has figured out how to do it.

The Iron Butt Association's most often read document is the "Archive of Wisdom," a collection of 29 tips on setting up the mind, body, and motorcycle for a long-distance ride. While our Archive of Wisdom page is a wonderful collection of intelligence and advice, I am often bombarded with requests for even more information. How do you select and prepare a motorcycle for long hours in the saddle? How do you prepare yourself, both mentally and physically, for longer rides?

My answer invariably begins, "It would take a book to answer all your questions." Today, we have that book in *Going the Extra Mile*. Ron, drawing on his own experience and that of a host of other long-distance enthusiasts, has succeeded in putting together *the* must-read book for riders seeking to learn the art of the long-distance ride. Enjoy!

Michael Kneebone, President
Iron Butt Association

Introduction

I've always enjoyed long automobile trips, so when I bought my first motorcycle in 1987, at the relatively mature age of 43, I wasn't terribly surprised to find that I enjoyed taking long motorcycle trips. What I *was* surprised to learn is the degree to which you can improve your comfort, safety, and enjoyment during long rides. The knowledge didn't come easily—or quickly.

Soon after buying my first motorcycle, I read about the Iron Butt Rally, a long-distance competition in which motorcyclists cover 1,000 miles or more per day for 11 consecutive days. Although the notion of covering such incredible distances on a motorcycle seemed impossible at the time, I began fantasizing about the possibility of participating in the rally some day.

A few years later I was returning to my home in Texas from a trip to Wisconsin. I traveled the 1,125 miles from my home to Wisconsin in less than 24 hours, had rested for a few days, and was attempting to repeat the feat on my way home.

I'd stopped at a service station along an interstate highway near Kansas City. It was a very hot July day, the sun was beating down on me, and it was nearly 100 degrees. I was mounted on a BMW K100RS sport tourer, dressed in a short-sleeved T-shirt, a pair of jeans, helmet, gloves, and cowboy boots. My leather jacket was secured to the rear seat of the motorcycle with bungie cords.

As I was refueling the motorcycle while gulping down a second bottle of Gatorade, a rider mounted on a BMW touring motorcycle pulled beside me, apparently interested in greeting a fellow BMW enthusiast. "Sure is a hot one, isn't it?" the rider asked as he flipped his face shield open and smiled. He was dressed from head-to-toe in what appeared to be a very hot, thickly padded riding suit. My shirt was soaked with perspiration, sweat was running down my face, and I thought about how incredibly fashion conscious this guy must be to be enduring all those fancy riding clothes. It was difficult to restrain myself from laughing or from making a good-natured but cynical comment about his garb. I considered asking him if he was cold or whether someone had just given him the motorcycle and riding outfit for his birthday, but I resisted the temptation.

The rider inquired about my destination and we exchanged a few pleasantries. I continued to try to slake my thirst as he took a few sips through a tube attached to a water bottle on his back. I'm sure that I chuckled to myself, once I replaced my helmet and was on my way. When I returned home, I related the incident to my riding buddies, most of whom rode cruisers and seldom traveled more than a few hundred miles a day. We had a good laugh at the anonymous rider's expense.

For all the fun I had telling the story to my friends, I can only imagine now what an interesting topic our encounter could have made as my unknown acquaintance described our meeting to *his* friends. Undoubtedly, experienced riders would have been entertained by his account of having met a middle-aged rider mounted on a $10,000 motorcycle, who was, except for a helmet, dressed totally inappropriately for the conditions.

It wasn't until several years later that I understood that this unknown rider had exhibited evidence that he was very experienced and knew how to be safe *and* comfortable while riding in the heat. He was undoubtedly more comfortable than me, yet at the time I would have insisted that the opposite was true. I don't know how he would have concealed his amusement if I had told him I was aspiring to participate in an Iron Butt Rally.

I could have profited from a good book describing how to prepare myself and my motorcycle for long, safe, comfortable, and enjoyable rides under extreme weather conditions—hot and cold, wet and dry. If I hadn't at least seen the September 1991 issue of *Motorcyclist,* in which long-distance enthusiast Jan Cutler described the best ten items for a long, fast ride, I'm confident I wouldn't have successfully completed my first Iron Butt Rally. Jan's half-page sidebar, which is still filed away in my desk drawer, was the only professional advice I had to go on before I participated in my first endurance event.

Today, after having competed in numerous long-distance competitions—including two Iron Butt Rallies—and after having written a few books on the subject of motorcycle endurance riding, novice riders frequently ask me basic questions. Whenever I'm asked what seems to be an obvious question, or when I see a rider who clearly hasn't learned the basic tricks for handling long distances, I reflect back on my own naivete.

Although this book includes a section on competitive rallies, it's not just about endurance riding. It's intended to help motorcyclists—beginners as well as experienced riders—learn how to ride long distances comfortably, safely, and more enjoyably.

CHAPTER 1

Comfort

Comfort is key to riding distances safely. To spend more time on your motorcycle, you must be prepared to ride in inclement weather and you should know how to adapt to extremes of heat and cold. You should learn how to make your motorcycle more comfortable and how to look after yourself on long trips. After long hours in the saddle, minor irritations drain energy and alertness. All riders can benefit from small modifications that enhance comfort and reduce fatigue.

You have more to gain by learning how to be comfortable on your motorcycle for longer periods than you do by riding at breakneck speed or riding while exhausted. As veteran Iron Butt competitor Bob Ray says, "Find out what makes you want to get off your bike, then fix it."

Riding Gear

When riders acquire their first motorcycle, they may add little more to their wardrobe than a helmet and some gloves. If they confine their riding to good weather, daylight, and only a few hundred miles per day, they may never feel the need for much more. Street clothing, however, is generally unsuitable for long rides. It doesn't provide sufficient protection from wind and rain nor from heat and cold. If you aspire to taking longer trips, you'll want to add riding boots, a rain suit, and perhaps a warmer jacket and pants. As you continue to build your daily mileage, you will be spending more time riding at night and in inclement weather, and you will begin to appreciate the convenience of an all-weather riding suit and the benefits of electric clothing.

Proper riding gear is as critical to your safety as it is to your well-being. Not only will it be your first line of defense against a potentially harsh environment, it has to protect you if you are unintentionally and unexpectedly introduced to the pavement. Seek out quality equipment that fits you well; if you don't select protective clothing that is *comfortable*, you may not wear it when you should.

The four key items needed for safe and comfortable long-distance riding are a helmet, boots, gloves, and a riding suit.

Helmet

I'm a vehement defender of your right to decide for yourself whether you wish to wear a helmet. Nevertheless, I don't know any serious riders who ride without them, even where there aren't

Iron Butt competitor Bill Thweatt's "ride-friendly" helmet attracts a lot of smiles. The only problem he has experienced is that children in the vehicles he passes seem to be encouraging their parents to speed up and follow him.

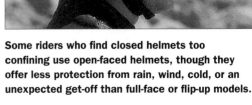

Some riders who find closed helmets too confining use open-faced helmets, though they offer less protection from rain, wind, cold, or an unexpected get-off than full-face or flip-up models.

The Schuberth Concept Helmet has an integrated, retractable sun visor that eliminates the need for sunglasses. This feature is especially useful when riding in the mountains during early morning or late afternoon, when you repeatedly pass from bright, sunny areas to dark shadows.

mandatory helmet laws. The majority of long-distance riders use full-face helmets, not only for the superior protection they offer during a get-off, but because they shield you from wind buffeting, rain, and other airborne objects, including insects. Full-face helmets are also ideal for the installation of helmet speaker systems.

Flip-up helmets allow you to eat, drink, and conduct a conversation without removing your helmet. Since this helmet doesn't have an integrated sun visor, the rider has put a couple of strips of electrical tape at the top of the faceshield.

In recent years, many riders have come to prefer the convenience of "flip-up" helmets, in which the face shield and chin bar can be raised without removing the helmet from your head. Glasses (including sunglasses) may be donned or removed, and you can eat, drink, smoke, chew, and conduct a conversation without taking off your helmet—a great convenience when it comes to streamlining pit stops. Flip-up helmets lack the structural integrity of full-face models, but they offer more protection than open-face helmets. I've owned a variety of helmets over the years, including different flip-up models. The Schuberth Concept Helmet fits my head well and its design incorporates many practical and innovative features I consider important:

- You can open the front by pressing a single button located on the left side of the helmet, so it isn't necessary to remove your right hand from the accelerator.

- You can get the helmet on and off without having to first remove your glasses, and there is enough clearance for you to wear glasses comfortably.

- Sunglasses are unnecessary, as an integral sun visor can be extended or retracted via a slide located on the left side of the helmet.

- The removable, washable inner lining of anti-allergenic fabric helps to prevent head itch.

- A unique face-shield ventilation system ratchets into five positions between open and closed. In addition, there are two grips at the top of the face shield, one on each side. When pressed forward, the shield can be offset slightly from the helmet, even when it's fully closed. During misty or rainy conditions, this circulating air helps to keep the shield from fogging.

Riding Suit

With the exception of your motorcycle, a quality riding suit will be one of the most expensive investments you will make. Traditional leather and denim might work fine if you limit outings to nice weather and warm climates, but long-distance riders will find themselves exposed to a variety of conditions—often unexpectedly—and they have to be prepared for anything they might encounter.

Even more important than guarding you from the elements, a good riding suit should protect your body in case of an accident. The best suit designs integrate soft, moldable pieces of body armor or padding to absorb impact in a crash. These components can often be easily removed for washing. Body armor is also available separately, if you would like to add it to the system you currently use. The Tri-Armor system from Motoport can be custom fitted and installed into virtually any jacket and pants.

Although leather competition suits offer the best protection against abrasion, few long-distance riders favor them. Since they aren't waterproof, you'll have to carry a rainsuit with you. There are many good rainsuits on the market, but they are a nuisance on long trips. For a rainsuit to be effective, you must stop and put it on before it rains, so you aren't putting it on over wet clothing. After it stops raining, you can never be sure whether to stop and remove it, or leave it on to avoid tempting fate. Although it will undoubtedly keep you dry, the coated nylon used in many rainsuits prevents perspiration from escaping, making you feel clammy. Fortunately, modern textile suits made of durable, breathable, high-tech fabrics not only eliminate most of these problems, they offer many unique features that have made them popular among long-distance enthusiasts.

One-piece suits. One-piece riding suits offer excellent protection and convenience for motorcyclists, and are especially popular among commuters who can slip them on and off easily over street clothing. Zippered vents along the torso, across the shoulders, and at the hips can make regulating temperature easier on hot days without sacrificing protection. Strategically

Bob Hall

Bob Hall won the 2001 Iron Butt Rally after an incredible third-leg ride from Sunnyside, Washington, to Madison, Alabama—via Prudhoe Bay, Alaska, the northernmost community in North America. Bob accomplished the 7,500-mile ride—1,000 miles on unpaved roads—in less than six-and-a-half days.

Bob was one of only three veteran riders who opted for the 1,000,000-point Prudhoe Bay bonus. He was the only rider to make it back to Madison before the final checkpoint closed. Although the Iron Butt Rally was Bob's first endurance win, he's competed in at least a dozen other rallies, including the Alberta 2000, the Waltz Across Texas, the Butt Lite, and the Minnesota 1000.

Bob believes the proper choice of clothing is one of the most important aspects of being able to ride long distances. "Most modern motorcycles are reliable and can run many tens of thousands of miles without problems," Bob says. "Some motorcycles are more comfortable to ride than others, but when it comes to riding big miles, the real issue is not the bike, it's the rider and the choice of riding gear. Some riders are limited to a few thousand miles per year because they are slaves to fashion. Get a serious riding outfit and watch the miles start to pile up." ∎

placed reflective trim will increase your visibility to other motorists.

The Aerostich Roadcrafter, manufactured and marketed exclusively by Riderwearhouse, is one of the most popular riding suits among long-distance veterans. Advertised as "a suitcase you can wear," the suit has an inner pocket with a Velcro closure for storage of valuables, a breast pocket for your gloves, and nine additional exterior pockets, including a small one on the right wrist for storing currency, coins, and credit cards. Like other suits from Riderwearhouse, the Roadcrafter is available in a wide range of colors and men's sizes. Women and those men who cannot wear standard sizes can custom order a suit to fit.

The Aerostich Roadcrafter has only one shortcoming: there are no storm flaps to protect the zippers. Depending on the severity of the rain and the amount of protection provided by your motorcycle's fairing and windshield, the zippers may leak after hours of wet weather. Although the Gore-Tex fabric itself won't leak, the water that seeps in at the zippers will eventually wick its way through to your clothing. The suit is so highly regarded by many high-mileage riders, however, that they carry a lightweight rain suit to wear over the Roadcrafter during heavy rain.

Two-piece suits. Many riders prefer the flexibility of a two-piece suit, as you can wear the top by itself when you are done riding. I appreciate this even more since I've started tent camping, as it's nice to shuck my overpants and lounge around camp in just my jacket, without having to pack extra outerwear. In addition, some people may be able to get a better overall fit from a two-piece suit than they would from a one-piece garment. Among long-distance riders, the Aerostich Darien, First Gear Kilimanjaro, and similar suits from Motoport and Tourmaster have their fans. Most of these jackets have an in-

Al Holtsberry, an Iron Butt Rally finisher in 1986 and 2001, selected this distinctive, white warm-weather riding suit for the start of the 2001 rally. Many high-mileage veterans own several riding outfits for different riding conditions.

sulated liner that can be removed in warmer weather. The Motoport Ultra II Kevlar suit is unique in that it incorporates chest plates in the body armor.

Boots

Unless you're fashion conscious or intend to spend a lot of time riding off the pavement, it isn't necessary to restrict your selection of boots to those made specifically for motorcycling. I haven't found any motorcycling boots that satisfy all of my requirements. Most of them have non-slip soles that provide traction on wet or oily surfaces and many are sturdy enough to provide protection in case of an accident. But most won't keep my feet warm while riding in sub-freezing temperatures, won't keep them dry while riding for hours in heavy rain, and aren't comfortable enough for extended wear off the motorcycle. For riders with "non-standard" sized feet, motorcycle boots often come only in limited sizes and widths.

One of my favorite boots is the Red Wing Style 1229, which is available in a variety of sizes and widths. At ten inches high, it's tall

This First Gear Kilimanjaro jacket includes armor padding that may be removed when the jacket is washed. The suit is available with standard padding, or with optional, heavy-duty padding.

enough so your pants won't creep up over the top of the boot. Constructed of red maple fortitude leather, the Red Wing has 1000 grams of Thinsulate, a built-in Gore-Tex bootie, and a non-slip Vibram sole that gives good traction. The robust insulation not only keeps my feet warm during freezing temperatures, it also protects them from the scorching temperatures I encounter on hot Texas summer days. As an added bonus, the boot is comfortable for walking.

Iron Butt competitor Marsha Hall used a two-piece Motoport suit during the 2001 Iron Butt rally. The Motoport Ultra II Kevlar outfit provides chest armor in addition to armor in the shoulders and elbows to protect the rider in the event of an accident.

Leathers are stylish, comfortable, and offer good abrasion resistance, but they generally aren't waterproof. It will be necessary to pack a rainsuit if you plan to continue riding after the rain begins. Also, leathers should provide for some ventilation or they can be uncomfortable on a hot day.

Many riders have found that it isn't necessary to restrict their selection of footwear to motorcycling-specific boots. The Red Wing style 1229 is insulated, waterproof, and high enough to offer good support and protection.

Gauntlets on gloves prevent cool air and rain from entering a rider's sleeve. Some riders prefer to put the gauntlets under the cuffs of their riding suit. As long as their arms are pointing down, the water doesn't enter their sleeves.

Riders who are particularly hard to fit may be interested in ordering made-to-measure motorcycle boots from Viberg Boot Manufacturing. Their boots have been recommended highly by several friends in the long-distance community.

Motorcycle endurance rider Norm Babcock was greeted warmly upon his arrival in Tonopah, Nevada, for the 2001 White Stag Rally, the endurance community's first rally of the year. Because of the heavy snow, the 2001 event was held in the lounge of the Station House Motel. Riders who contend with such conditions must know how to avoid hypothermia.

If your favorite riding boots are not waterproof, you'll need to purchase a pair of rubber Totes or coated nylon overboots that you can slip on when it is raining. Boot coverings are inexpensive, don't take up much room, and will keep your feet dry. As with rainsuits, they're also a bit of a nuisance, and most types are not sturdy enough to hold up to a lot of walking.

Gloves

Some novices seem to believe that gloves fall into the same category as helmets: they offer protection in case of an accident, but it's more comfortable to ride without them. Gloves are necessary to shield your hands from sun, cold, stones and other flying objects. At 60 miles an hour, just being struck by an insect can be painful. Gloves are especially beneficial if you should ever go down, even at low speed, as it's instinctive to extend your hands to break your fall. Some riders experience numbness in their hands from vibrations transmitted through the handlebars, and wearing gloves will provide some insulation from the vibration. You may find your hands tire less easily as well.

You should have three weights of gloves: lightweight, short deerskin gloves for summer use; middleweight, unlined leather gauntlet gloves for cooler weather; and heavy, waterproof leather gauntlet gloves for cold or wet weather.

Lightweight deerskin summer gloves are a little warmer than textile gloves, but they offer more protection if you take a fall. For cooler weather, the middleweight gauntlet gloves will prevent cold air from rushing up your sleeves. The heavy, waterproof gloves will be used in cold weather, and are also designed to prevent cold air or rain from entering your riding suit.

Gloves such as the Olympia Ultima are insulated and have a waterproof liner. They also have a Kevlar reinforced palm and padded, raised knuckles. In my experience, they will stay dry for up to several hours of heavy rain. I haven't found a totally satisfactory solution to gloves eventually getting wet, however. If you carry several pairs of gloves, you can put on a dry pair when the ones you're wearing become uncomfortable.

I'm usually quite happy to ride with wet hands as long as they are warm; with heated handgrips, my hands have seldom been too cold. When the rain eventually stops, I place the wet gloves into a mesh bag on the back of my motorcycle and let them dry. If you don't have a "wet bag," simply fasten them under a luggage strap or bungie cord.

Some riders cover their gloves during rain, with either rubber plumber's gloves or waterproof nylon overmitts. You'll have to experiment for yourself to see what will work for you. I know riders who find glove covers to be a good solution, but I've never liked using them, as I don't feel as comfortable with the controls.

Staying Warm

The vast majority of riders in northern climates winterize their motorcycles in the fall and don't bring them out of the garage again until late spring or summer. Some ardent enthusiasts continue to use their motorcycles all year long, however, even in the north country. But even motorcyclists who don't intend to ride in the cold are sometimes caught unaware by a sudden drop in the temperature. Many riders also underestimate the effect of the windchill factor resulting from the speed of a moving motorcycle (see sidebar).

It's possible to make some very enjoyable trips during freezing temperatures if you have

Radar detectors are not typically waterproof. Carolyn "Skert" Youorski provides hers with a plastic cover that was originally designed to protect instruments on boats. As with many rally-equipped motorcycles, Skert's BMW 1150GS sports two GPS receivers: the Garmin III Plus and a Garmin Street Pilot. The small device next to the GPS receivers is an MP3 player that provides music through her headphone speakers.

A necessity for long trips, this Helen TwoWheels wet bag provides a convenient way to dry gear while riding.

proper clothing and equipment to remain warm. Riding when you're cold, however, can be uncomfortable and annoying, sapping your resources and attention. Taken to its extreme, it can result in hypothermia, an especially dangerous situation for a motorcyclist.

Hypothermia is a gradual and insidious debility that overtakes you in stages. Your body temperature falls, your natural responses grow sluggish, and you become disoriented. A person suffering hypothermia progresses from mild to increasingly violent shivering as the body tries to warm itself with muscular contractions. It leads to extreme weariness, heaviness of movement, a distorted sense of time and distance, and increasing confusion resulting in a tendency to make imprudent and illogical decisions. If permitted to persist, the mind grows disoriented and subject to hallucinations—including the misconception that you aren't cold but that you're on fire. Shivering ceases, the body gives up, and apathy prevails.

Temperature (degrees F)

Wind (mph)	40	30	20	10	0	-10	-20	-30	-40
40	27	13	-1	-15	-29	-43	-57	-71	-84
50	26	12	-3	-17	-31	-45	-60	-74	-88
60	25	10	-4	-19	-33	-48	-62	-76	-91
70	24	9	-6	-20	-35	-49	-64	-79	-93
80	23	8	-7	-21	-36	-51	-66	-81	-96
90	22	7	-8	-23	-38	-53	-68	-83	-98

Frostbite occurs in 15 minutes or less

If you are cold and begin to recognize these warning signs, stop as soon as possible and do whatever is necessary to get warm. If you can't purchase additional clothing, take a motel room and start again in the morning, or alternate your riding with frequent warm-up stops.

The accompanying table, provided by the National Oceanic and Atmospheric Administration, describes the effective temperature resulting from the combined effect of wind (or motorcycle speed) and ambient temperature.

Layering

The most important key to remaining warm is to be "loose and layered." Clothing that is too tight constricts circulation and doesn't insulate well, since it can't trap air which will keep you warm. Multiple layers of loose clothing increase the dead air space surrounding your body. Individual pieces of clothing may then be added or removed as appropriate for varying weather conditions.

Your innermost layers of clothing should consist of a material that draws moisture away from the body, dries quickly, and will continue to insulate, even when wet. Cotton is not recommended for inner garments because it retains moisture and will conduct heat away from your body when it's damp. In addition to long-johns in varying weights of polypropylene, any good outdoor retailer will also stock socks and glove liners, which can add a layer of warmth and comfort to any system.

On a cool day, you will need to wear an insulating middle layer between your inner and outer

This common-looking jacket and pants from Gerbing are actually two of the warmest items of electric clothing available. Designed to be worn under a riding suit, each piece can be fitted with an independent thermostat, so you can control the warmth of each garment separately. Heated clothing like this can greatly extend the range of conditions in which you can ride comfortably.

layers of clothing, to both retain the heat generated by your body and keep out the cold. Choices of material include wool, polyester pile or compressed polyester fleece, or spun synthetic filaments, such as Dacron, Hollofil II, Polyguard, or Thinsulate. Wool absorbs moisture but continues to insulate when wet. Polyester pile or compressed polyester fleece is similar to wool in structure, but pound for pound it is thicker and warmer.

By definition, your riding gear will make up your outer layer of clothing, and it will bear most of the responsibility for keeping out the rain and cold. On a very cold day, try wearing a lightweight ski mask or balaclava beneath your helmet. Full-face helmets sometimes leak cold air around the vents, and you may find it best to duct tape over these drafts if it is really raw out. To keep your toes warm in an emergency, don a vapor barrier (such as a plastic trash bag) over your wicking layer; although your feet won't be able to "breathe," they will be more comfortable than if they are frozen.

Seamans Jones, an Iron Butt Rally veteran who has lived in Anchorage, Alaska, for almost 30 years, has tried just about everything to keep his feet warm. During his riding career, he's experimented with multiple layers of socks, battery-operated hunting socks, chemical packs, and electrically heated insoles. He insists that Gerbing's electric socks are the way to go, worn over socks and sock liners. Seamans also recommends using a good pair of waterproof, insulated boots a half-size larger than you normally wear.

Electric Clothing

When the core of the body (the chest and organs) becomes chilled, blood flow is restricted to the extremities, preserving heat for the vital organs. So long as the torso remains toasty, the body will continue to pump warm blood to the fingers and toes. Because of this, one of the most effective items of cold-weather clothing for motorcyclists is an electric vest or heated jacket. Electric gloves, socks, chaps, and pants may also help you remain comfortable in freezing temperatures.

Many motorcyclists either don't know there is such a thing as electric clothing for motor-

Gore-Tex vs. Vapor-Barrier Clothing

Most textile riding suits use Gore-Tex or a similar "breathable" membrane bonded to the outer material layer, because it should permit moisture from perspiration to escape, while preventing rain from penetrating the fabric. However, since perspiration will pass through, so too will wind, which means that Gore-Tex garments are not windproof. In cold weather, this shortcoming may be overcome by wearing additional insulation beneath your riding suit.

Advocates of vapor-barrier clothing argue that it's better to wear a non-porous material as the outer layer, even though perspiration cannot escape from it. It's better to go ahead and sweat, the argument goes, than to be cold under a Gore-Tex outer layer. The vapor-barrier advocates suggest wearing a non-porous rainsuit as an outer layer because it will provide the best protection against the wind. Though it seems to be warmer, friends who have tried vapor-barrier clothing report feeling "clammy" after wearing it for extended periods. ∎

cycling, or haven't experienced the joy of using it. It's the ultimate remedy for cold-weather riding. Your motorcycle's electrical system provides current to the clothing; some touring motorcycles are equipped with an electrical accessory socket that you can plug into. Alternately, an adapter can be mounted directly to the motorcycle's battery. If you're riding a late-model touring motorcycle, your bike probably has sufficient electrical capacity to power electric clothing. If you have any doubts, consult your shop manual or dealer to determine how much power your motorcycle needs to function compared to how much it generates.

For many riders, a heated vest or jacket liner is all that's needed. One of the things I like most about my electric vest is the heated collar, which extends up under my helmet and protects the back of my neck from the cold. Several manufacturers make chaps or wired pants that can be either regulated independently with a separate heat controller, or connected to the vest and operated from the same thermostat. The legs of my chaps are long enough that I stuff them into my boots to help warm my feet.

Although many riders keep their hands warm with heavy insulated gloves and heated grips, heated gloves are also available, as are electric socks—both of which are best used with a thermostat that is separated from your other electric clothing.

Staying Cool

It's easier for a motorcyclist to stay warm than to stay cool. You can wear additional clothing or plug in an electric vest, but you can't buy refrigerated clothing. When temperatures soar, it's more difficult to make yourself comfortable while wearing the protection you'll need in case of a mishap. The foolish react by riding in shirtsleeves, sometimes without a helmet.

You must understand that it's important to wear clothing to stay cool, even in scorching temperatures. Keeping your riding suit on will help your body retain moisture and avoid dehydration. Riders who shed protective clothing place greater stress on their bodies than those who stay dressed and modify their behavior for the extreme heat. If you doubt this, consider residents of the deserts of Africa and the Middle East, who wrap themselves in protective clothing while riding camels across the desert. Keeping your riding suit on provides another important advantage: you'll still have some protection if you go down.

Some manufacturers of riding apparel offer clothing with ventilated leather or metal mesh panels meant to maximize airflow without sacrificing all protection. Although garments like this

Left and top right The Aerostich Roadcrafter has ventilation openings beneath the arms, as well as wide ventilation flaps across the shoulders. By opening these vents along with the front of the jacket, a rider will enjoy the benefit of cross-ventilation.

Bottom right The First Gear Kilimanjaro jacket has a ventilation flap across the shoulders and ventilation through the sleeves and at the chest. Quality riding suits provide ventilation at the front and the back of the suit.

can be useful for day rides, I avoid single-purpose pieces of gear for longer trips.

Quality riding suits are typically equipped with several strategically placed vents. If you unzip the front of your riding suit nearly to the waist and open the vents, air entering the front of the suit and exiting through the vents will provide some cooling. Things should be bearable as long as you're moving. Don't forget to open the ventilation slots on your helmet as well.

Though it should go without saying, you must drink plenty of water in hot weather to stay hydrated.

The Bottom Line

When things get really steamy, some riders develop a painful affliction of the posterior known as "monkey butt," named for the colorful nature of the condition. You can avoid developing the rash by keeping your skin dry with the application of Gold Bond powder. Before taking off in the morning, sprinkle the powder liberally under your armpits and between your toes too.

Bad underwear can also spawn a host of discomforts, especially after sitting on a motorcycle all day. Avoid seams and excess material that can chafe and restrict circulation. Modern wicking fabrics are ideal materials from which to fashion such base layer garments, since they help to transfer moisture from your skin, so you will stay more comfortable. Most synthetic fibers are hydrophobic, meaning they don't absorb moisture. When washed in a motel sink, they dry quickly so you can pack fewer changes of clothing.

Riderwearhouse offers CoolMax undergarments with flat seams designed to eliminate bunching and chafing.

Get Wet

When temperatures get really extreme, as could be the case if you're crossing the Mojave Desert at noon in July, give yourself the advantage of evaporative cooling by wetting yourself down. Pour water over your neck and permit it to drench your shirt. Depending on the temperature and humidity, the cooling effect could last a long time.

Dave McQueeney

In 2000, the "I've Been Everywhere Tour" challenged riders to visit the 92 cities, towns, and hamlets mentioned in the country western classic song, "I've Been Everywhere." The song's lyrics included such remote locations as Barranquilla, Colombia; Chatanika, Alaska; Schefferville, Quebec; and Dynamita, Mexico. Of the more than 200 entrants, Dave McQueeney was the only rider to visit all 92 locations between mid-April and mid-October.

In addition to completing the Iron Butt Rally (IBA membership #30), Dave has completed the Four Corners Tour—on *four* different motorcycles. After riding to each of the four corners of the continental United States, Dave returned to his home in Los Angeles and exchanged motorcycles before heading for the next corner.

Dave received an award from the BMWMOA at the 2001 Iron Butt gathering in Daytona in recognition of having documented more than 1,000,000 miles on BMW motorcycles.

Dave learned long ago that one key to remaining comfortable during rides is to not sit on anything that can press into his skin. "I don't sit on a wallet, a seat with thick stitching, or clothing with seams against my skin," Dave says. "Anything that exerts pressure will impair circulation and eventually become painful." ■

Cowboys discovered the benefit of wet bandanas centuries ago. If you can cool the large blood vessels that pass through your neck on the way to the heart, it helps your whole body feel cooler. Today, special wraps designed to retain moisture, such as the Kool-Off Tie sold by Riderwearhouse, are designed specifically for this purpose.

Taking evaporative cooling one step further, special vests available from Ride Cool and Marsee are meant to be soaked in water, then worn against the body. When wearing a wet vest, adjust the ventilation of your riding suit to get sufficient cooling without drying out the vest too quickly. The consensus among many desert riders is that vests work well. During high humidity, however, some users report that they are a bit clammy.

Keep a Cool Head

Once, during a long, hot trip through south Texas, I had an inspiration. After parking my bike at a gas pump, I removed my helmet and placed it into the sidewalk freezer that held the store's supply of bagged ice. By the time I refueled, paid for the purchase, and drank a bottle of cold water, the helmet had cooled nicely. The effect lasted a long time. In a similar vein, some riders stuff the pockets of their riding suits with ice to get some relief from the heat.

If you spend much time riding in very hot climates, a tinted face shield will keep the temperature inside your helmet a few degrees cooler. Also, if your helmet doesn't have a removable, washable liner, consider using a separate helmet liner of silk or CoolMax, which is designed to wick away perspiration to keep you more comfortable. By washing your helmet liner regularly, you'll also prolong the life and user-friendliness of your lid. Helmet liners are available at many motorcycle shops and from most motorcycle catalogues.

Body Care

It isn't necessary to be a world-class athlete to ride long distances, or even to compete in endurance rallies. But you'll be more comfortable riding the extra miles if you're in good physical condition than if you're overweight and unaccustomed to physical exertion. Your body will be operating a little closer to its peak efficiency—a key ingredient to stamina. Although I don't usually take time to exercise during a competitive event, when I'm on an extended tour I've sometimes packed a jump rope, which is compact and can give you a good workout in only 15 minutes or so.

Your choice of foods can also have a significant impact on both your stamina and your ability to delay the onset of fatigue. If you choose wisely, it's possible to eat relatively healthy, even on gasoline station food. Competitive endurance riders invest a lot of attention to following rigorous eating programs designed to maximize energy during extended rides. These specialized regimens are discussed further in Chapter 5: Getting Competitive.

Eliminating Irritants

When you are putting in a long day in the saddle, minor irritations of wind, weather, and vibration

Bryce Ulrich

While working at Microsoft, Bryce Ulrich was a program manager for handheld and palm-size PCs running Windows CE. He left the company to re-energize himself and to see the United States and Canada from the seat of his motorcycle. Bryce's goals were to complete a Four Corners Tour, visit as many national parks as possible, and visit all 50 states and the Canadian provinces.

Bryce completed his 50-state ride on the twisty road to Hana on the island of Maui in Hawaii. In addition to the Four Corners tour and his 50-state ride, Bryce has completed several IBA rides, including two Iron Butt Rallies.

For hot weather riding, Bryce is an advocate of cooling vests. He keeps his vest folded in a zip-lock bag, pours water into the bag, and shakes and kneads it for 30 seconds. If it's very hot, he doesn't wring the excess water from the vest. When he takes the vest off, he folds it into a mesh bag and straps it to the outside of the motorcycle so that it will dry and air out. ■

can really add up. With a just little bit of diligence, however, you can minimize discomforts and eliminate irritants that will distract and fatigue you. There are a few inexpensive but essential items you will find in every rider's kit. Carry lip balm, sunscreen, eyewash, and insect repellant in your tankbag or jacket so they will be readily available when needed.

Even with a full-face helmet, your lips can become dry and cracked; remember to reapply lip balm regularly at your pit stops. If your eyes become dry and irritated, carry eyewash too. Sunburn lotion can keep your face from taking on the look of a raccoon. If you don't use gloves with gauntlets, remember to apply sunscreen to your wrists too; it will prevent a painful "burn band" where your skin is exposed.

Although you won't have to worry about mosquitoes while you're moving, a good insect repellent can be a godsend when you make pit stops or stop for a nap at a roadside rest area. Before dozing off, put some mosquito repellent on any area of your skin that's exposed. If you camp while traveling, you'll find few campgrounds that are free of biting insects.

Earplugs. It's very important to protect your hearing while riding a motorcycle. If your hearing sounds muffled after riding, or if your ears ring, then you are suffering temporary hearing damage. If repeated regularly, the damage could become permanent.

Even if earplugs weren't needed to prevent gradual hearing loss, they greatly reduce aural fatigue. Once you become accustomed to wearing earplugs, it's unlikely you'll want to ride without them. In instances when I've neglected to insert them, or haven't inserted them properly before starting a ride, the noise from the wind and the motorcycle is so aggravating that I stop to correct the situation.

Earplugs are either reusable or disposable, and there's a large variety of each type. It's easy to spend more for earplugs than necessary. I once tried a set of expensive, complicated ribbed plugs designed for musicians but they were so uncomfortable that I discarded them after using them only a few times. A similar looking pair purchased elsewhere with an even higher decibel

Asa McFadden

Before the Iron Butt Rally in 2001, Asa Mc Fadden was one of only three riders who had documented the IBA's Ultimate Coast-to-Coast Ride—from Key West, Florida, to Deadhorse (Prudhoe Bay), Alaska. Asa made the ride in 1996 and 1998, the last of which he completed in less than five days, eleven hours—the shortest time recorded for the ride.

In addition to his brief "let's diagonally slice the continent" ride, Asa has completed the Iron Butt Rally three times and has earned the IBA 10/10ths Award, the Bun Burner Gold Award, the Saddle Sore 2000 Award, and the Saddle Sore 5000 Award.

Lifeguards, who must spend a lot of time in the sun, often coat their noses with a heavy cream that blocks the sun's rays. Asa has developed a different approach for protecting his nose from the sun; he fashioned a mask from a piece of black vinyl. ∎

rating was less expensive and much more comfortable. Shop around and be prepared to experiment a little to find out what works for you. Many mail-order catalogs offer sample packs of assorted varieties of earplugs.

My favorite disposable models are the soft Hearos brand. If inserted properly, these provide the quietest seal, but they are sometimes difficult to extract if inserted too far into the ear canal. Although they are disposable, you can use them a few times before discarding them. Reusable, ribbed rubber earplugs are also comfortable and seal well; wash them frequently to ward off infection from dirt.

Earplugs can be purchased in quantities, so you can save a little money on the cost per pair. You can sometimes find a Super Value Pack of Hearos at your local discount pharmacy. Lab Safety Supply, Inc. also markets a vast quantity of different types of earplugs, both disposable and reusable, which can be ordered over the Internet. Many types come attached to a cord, so you can leave them hanging around your neck when you remove them.

If you're interested in the high end, you can have earplugs custom molded to the shape of your ear. Some models can be made with embedded speakers for use with your motorcycle's sound system or a portable cassette or CD player. Many riders prefer integrated speakers because they don't have to modify an expensive helmet to accommodate regular speakers, and the sound is usually excellent. For more on this, see the section on Sound Systems later in this chapter.

Eye care. Most people who find it necessary to correct their vision have several choices: they

Dave Barr

Dave Barr is an inspiration to motorcyclists and non-riders alike. A rugged, extraordinary adventurer, Dave is the only person to have ridden a Harley-Davidson motorcycle around the world—despite the loss of both legs from an antitank mine explosion in Angola. He skydives regularly and was the first double amputee skydiver in the world.

Dave Barr at the Arctic Circle in Norway. (courtesy of Dave Barr)

His global odyssey, from September 1990 to May 1994, covered six continents and more than 83,000 miles. Dave rode his motorcycle across the Sahara, Namib, and Gobi deserts. He circled the continent of Australia and negotiated the Andes during avalanche season. Not satisfied to stop after this accomplishment, Dave traveled from the Atlantic Ocean to the Pacific Ocean, across Europe, Russia, and Siberia. This 13,000-mile ride began in the winter of 1996 and earned him a place in the Guinness Book of World Records.

Dave is an inspirational speaker who has addressed major international business corporations, military groups, public service organizations, and charitable foundations throughout the world. He maintains a web site at www.davebarr.com.

Whether at home or on the road, Dave adheres to a strict daily exercise regimen. His routine includes jumping jacks (from the waist up), pushups, riding a stationary bicycle, and use of a small roller device that he uses on the floor to exercise his upper body. Even when he's traveling, he takes the roller with him and performs his calisthenics. ■

can wear eyeglasses or contact lenses, or they can sometimes choose surgery to correct their problem, or they can use some combination of these strategies. Vanity notwithstanding, some people are simply not good candidates for surgery (or contacts) and contact lenses typically require some nominal care and upkeep, even if you are using the extended-wear variety. Eyeglasses, however, can also be a bit of a hassle, especially when you add a full-face motorcycle helmet into the equation, as you usually have to take them off every time you remove and replace your helmet. Glasses can also get dirty or fogged. If you have needed vision correction all your life, you have probably already weighed these compromises and arrived at a solution you are happy with.

Even riders blessed with good vision in their youth may find themselves suffering from presbyopia as they enter their forties, a condition whereby you have difficulty seeing both near and far objects—a nuisance for motorcyclists who must be able to read their instruments and see at a distance. The most common strategy for dealing with this involves traditional bifocals and trifocals, though "progressive" lenses have become very popular. In this last case, the lens has a graduated field of focus and the wearer subtly adjusts the position of his head to find the correction they need at any given focal length. Riders who are pleased with progressive lenses typically report that they work best if you ex-

A one-gallon water jug can be quickly and easily outfitted with a drinking tube. The two small bottles stored in the pockets of the auxiliary fuel cell cover can be kept in reserve as an emergency backup supply.

plain to your optometrist how you plan to use them, so he can lower the near-focus field accordingly; otherwise you may find you have to tip your head back more than you'd want just to see your cockpit.

When it comes to correcting presbyopia, mono-vision lenses (contacts or eyeglasses) present an alternative to bifocals and the like. Using this technique, one eye is corrected for near vision, and the other for distance. Most people become adjusted to this type of system within

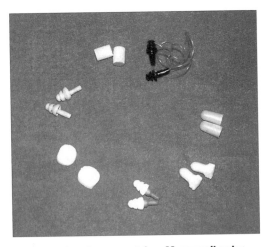

Earplugs come in many styles. Many mail-order companies offer sample packs of assorted varieties, so you can experiment and see what works best for you.

Integrated earplug speakers are very small and don't interfere with wearing a helmet. Advocates of earplug speakers say that the sound quality is much better than it is with helmet speakers. By hooking these earplug speakers into a cassette or CD player, you can listen to your favorite tunes while riding.

Left
Some riding suits allow you to insert a bota bag into a compartment at the rear of the jacket, making it easy to carry water while you're riding.

Right
The Kilimanjaro jacket has a built-in opening for routing a drinking tube where it can be accessed easily while riding.

a few days. I have used mono-vision contact lenses for more than ten years and I find they work great for me while avoiding all the trouble associated with reading glasses. Not only can I glance easily from my instruments to the horizon, I can also wear sunglasses if I choose. If mono-vision lenses would work for you, it is an option I recommend you explore.

That white cup below the left handlebar of Morris Kruemcke's Gold Wing is the business end of Morris's infamous "pee tube." Morris contends that since he doesn't worry about wasting time with frequent stops, he's less likely to refrain from drinking and become dehydrated.

Bright sun. When riding in the sun, many riders prefer to replace their helmet's clear face shield with a tinted one, rather than be bothered with sunglasses. You can store your spare face shield in an old sock in your tankbag. This system works well so long as you don't procrastinate about stopping to change face shields at sundown or sunrise.

Some riders use sunglasses so they don't have to pack an additional face shield. They consider it less troublesome to put on and remove sunglasses than to swap face shields. Of course, helmets with retractable sun visors make all these hassles obsolete. A retractable sun visor is especially useful in the mountains in the early morning or late evening when you're alternating between bright sunlight and darkness.

Kidney belts. Truck drivers and operators of heavy construction equipment find that the additional back support of a kidney belt helps to prevent back pain, since they keep your organs from bouncing around when your torso is subject to constant vibration, as it is when you are on a long motorcycle trip. Kidney belts are available from motorcycle shops and from sporting goods stores and athletic shops.

Meals on Wheels

Whenever I discuss long-distance riding, people invariably ask me how I eat on the road. My eating program varies depending on whether I'm at home, on a leisurely tour, or competing in a high-impact endurance event. At home, I eat modest-sized, balanced, low-fat meals at least four or five times per day.

While touring, it's inconvenient to stop to eat that often. Besides, I often look forward to a "more than modest size" dinner at the end of the day (like a nice T-bone steak with a baked potato and a few beers). During these trips, I usually start the day with a light breakfast (sometimes only fruit) and have a modest lunch, such as one of Subway's low-fat submarine sandwiches or a large salad and a baked potato from a soup and salad bar.

Iron Butt Association President Mike Kneebone prefers to stop occasionally for meals at restaurants that provide counter service, such as Denny's. He's developed a system that allows him to minimize wasted time while getting a healthier meal than is usually available from fast-food establishments. He claims to hold these stops to 20 or 30 minutes. "While your fellow riders are choking down a cold sandwich standing around a gasoline pump, you can have a relaxing hot meal," Mike contends.

If the restaurant is crowded, Mike sits at the counter. As soon as he can, he tells the waitress that he's in a hurry and would like his check delivered with his meal. He also gives the waitress a nice tip up front. Then, he orders a meal that he knows will be readily available or pre-cooked. For example, Mike claims that every Denny's in America can dish up ready-made spaghetti in a few minutes.

After Mike explains that he'll be back soon, he heads for the restroom to wash up. Even if he isn't dirty, he finds washing his face to be refreshing. This can also be a good time to reapply sunscreen or skin lotion, as needed. If he must make a phone call, he tries to do it with the dead time before his meal is delivered. By the time Mike returns, his meal is usually on the table.

Mike also cautions riders to think out meal stops. The Waffle House usually has fast service,

Michael Kneebone

Mike Kneebone participated in several early Iron Butt rallies in the late 1980s and became President of the Iron Butt Association in 1991. His personal riding accomplishments include setting several Guinness World Records, including New York to San Francisco in less than 48 hours, riding more than 1,700 miles in 24 hours, and riding a motorcycle to all 48 contiguous states in six days, thirteen hours, and twenty-one minutes. Although these records have since been broken, Mike continues to be recognized throughout the world as "Mr. Iron Butt" for his continuing contributions to safe long-distance riding.

Mike is best known as rallymaster of the Iron Butt Rally, "The World's Toughest Motorcycle Competition." The Iron Butt is a biennial event that takes place at the end of August in odd-numbered years. The rally has become so popular that beginning in 1997 it was necessary to award the approximately 100 entry positions through a drawing.

Mike has traveled throughout the world by motorcycle. In addition to extensive travels in North and South America, he circumnavigated Australia and has ridden in Europe and several Middle Eastern countries.

Mike recommends that during long trips, riders carry two sources of water—one for drinking whenever you are thirsty and another that should be reserved for emergencies. "The emergency supply should be stored in an area that is inconvenient to get to," Mike says. "You don't want to be tempted to use the backup supply unless you've broken down and have exhausted your main supply." ■

When it comes to the Iron Butt Rally, Mike Kneebone (with cap and clipboard) runs the show.

but if you arrive at 10 a.m. on a Sunday morning, you'll have to wait in line for a table.

Staying Hydrated

What you drink, and how often you drink, is as important as what you eat. Minor changes in the make-up of local water supplies can lead to upset stomach and diarrhea. In 1995 the federal government warned that cryptosporidium, a disease-carrying parasite, can slip through most municipal water treatment systems. While a healthy individual can fight off this bug, you can avoid such problems altogether by using bottled water.

When you drink *only* water for extended periods, however, your body will excrete minerals and salts in sweat and urine that must be replaced to avoid electrolyte imbalance. Many sports re-hydration solutions contain a good balance of fluid and electrolytes. Eating fruit (especially bananas) and drinking fruit juices will also help replace lost electrolytes.

Since you should be sipping water constantly throughout a day, it's important that your water supply be conveniently located so you will have no excuse for not drinking when you should. Hands-free hydration systems, like the popular CamelBak, can be carried on your back or in your tankbag. One riding suit, the First Gear Kilimanjaro, has a built-in pocket to hold a water bladder, as well as integral grommets through which you can route the drinking tube.

To ensure that sufficient water is available during long endurance runs, most riders equip their motorcycles with a half-gallon or more. During rallies when I'd prefer not to be stopping to refill a water bag, I mount a one-gallon jug on the rear seat. First, I drill a small hole through the plastic cap and insert one end of a long plastic tube into the top of the water container. A small piece of Velcro near the drinking end of the tube lets me affix it to the outside of the jug when I'm not sipping. It is important to ensure the tube isn't so long that it could become wrapped in the rear wheel if the Velcro becomes unattached.

If I fill the jug with ice before adding water, the liquid will remain cool for a surprisingly long time, even when I'm riding through the desert.

Balancing input and output. The key to remaining properly hydrated is to drink early and often enough so that you never feel thirsty—by then it's too late; you will have already lost important fluids and electrolytes and become dehydrated. In hot weather, sip water almost continuously. Even mild dehydration can bring

Left
Even though Keith Keating completed the 2001 Iron Butt Rally on this Suzuki GN 125, such lightweight motorcycles are not very comfortable, no matter what modifications are made to them. Also, it's often not possible to maintain legal highway speed limits on such a bike.

Right
IBR veteran Bob Ray ran the 2001 Iron Butt Rally on his Honda Reflex Scooter, a vehicle with only twice the engine displacement of Keith Keating's Suzuki GN 125. Despite the scooter's limitations, Ray finished the rally ahead of many competitors who were mounted on much larger, more powerful motorcycles.

about headache, fatigue, and muscle cramps—precisely the types of conditions you want to avoid while riding.

You can check your own hydration status: light colored urine means you're well hydrated; dark urine means you should increase your intake of water. You might be wondering if the benefit of drinking a lot of water would be offset, at least in part, by your having to stop frequently to urinate, but you'd be surprised how much water you can lose through perspiration. Though I usually drink steadily, I rarely need to use the restroom more often than the four or five hours between my usual fuel stops.

Balancing the intake and output of fluids takes some practice, as you carefully note the amount of water you're drinking. While riding through North American deserts during July and August, I've learned that I can take six or seven long sips from the jug whenever I detect a hint of thirst. In colder temperatures, I may take only two or three sips.

Note that caffeinated drinks will cause you to urinate more frequently, as caffeine is a mild diuretic. According to industry sources, 70 percent of soft drinks on the market contain some caffeine. Coffee and soft drinks are not the only sources of caffeine, however. Many over-the-counter cold remedies, such as Sudafed, contain ephedrine or ephedrine-like compounds that will also increase urination.

Riders who wish to cover all their bases can take a tip from veteran Iron Butt competitor Morris Kruemcke, designer of the infamous "pee-tube" mounted on his motorcycle which permits him to relieve himself without stopping. Morris has become almost as well-known in endurance-riding circles for his famous "pee-tube" as he is for having made some incredible rides (nearly 1,200 miles) without touching his feet to the ground.

If you're interested in purchasing a similar commercial item, the "E-Z Leaker" or the Liberated Spectator's "Stadium Pal" are available over the Internet. Although I don't have any first-hand experience with the devices, I understand they are available in several sizes and configurations, including female versions.

Bob Mutchler

When Bob Mutchler was only nine months old, he was stricken with the poliovirus and spent the next three years confined to an iron lung. His parents were told he had little hope of survival. Although he still suffers from paralysis in his legs and requires crutches and leg braces to walk, Bob is an accomplished motorcycle endurance rider who has completed two Iron Butt Rallies using a sidecar rig.

"In most cases, installing a sidecar renders a motorcycle less suitable for long-distance touring," Bob says. "In certain adverse circumstances, such as rainy nights, gusting crosswinds, frost, and muddy detours, the three-wheeler is easier to control, with the added benefit of not falling down. It also offers additional carrying capacity and low-speed maneuverability. But the larger, heavier vehicle requires more effort to ride most of the time."

Several years ago, Bob came up with a novel idea to turn his love of marathon motorcycling into a campaign for polio awareness. A Rotarian, Bob began participating in marathon motorcycle rides to help raise awareness for the Rotary Club's PolioPlus program and the eradication of polio.

In addition to being a proficient motorcyclist, Bob is an accomplished musician and owns a successful piano tuning and restoration business.

■

Motorcycle Modification

Comfort begins by matching the motorcycle to the rider. Most motorcycles can be modified to dramatically improve comfort on long-distance rides, though some are more comfortable to begin with. If you decide to get serious about long-distance riding, your interest will probably gravitate toward a large-displacement touring or sport-touring motorcycle, though large adventure touring machines like the BMW R1150 GS have their fans in the long-distance community. If you plan on touring two-up or carrying a lot of luggage and camping gear, you will need to pay particular attention to the Gross Vehicle Weight Rating of your motorcycle, to ensure it can safely accommodate the intended load. For more on this important topic, see Chapter 3: Trip Planning and Organization.

When it comes to long-distance riding, larger bikes typically have many advantages, including integrated luggage and the electrical capacity for powering auxiliary lights, heated clothing, and other accessories. Larger displacement engines, bigger windscreens and fairings, and factory installed communications systems also contribute to the suitability of larger bikes for long-distance touring.

In spite of this, experienced riders have demonstrated that you can achieve high mileage on just about any properly prepared motorcycle, although riders who rally on very small bikes usually do so to prove it can be done, not to finish high in the standings; Keith Keating completed the 2001 Iron Butt on a Suzuki GN 125. The point is, all bikes can be made more comfortable and the bike you currently own can get you started.

Peter Hoogeveen has competed successfully on a sport bike, garnering three Top Ten finishes in the Iron Butt Rally on a Honda CBR-XX, though he is virtually the only such highly-placed competitor in the last three events who

Peter Hoogeveen's consistent top finishes in major endurance-riding competitions have earned him a special position of prominence in the rally community. Peter is one of only a few riders to ride a sport bike. Here, he is being checked in at the end of the 2001 Iron Butt Rally.

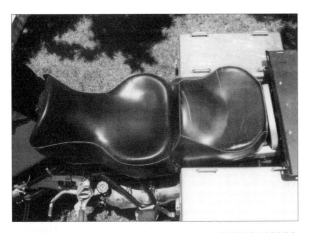

The driver's and passenger's seats on my BMW R1150GS were handmade by Bill Mayer Saddles for me and my wife. When you have a seat custom made, you can tailor it specifically to your personal riding style. Most custom seats are available with either a leather or vinyl covering.

Popular with many long-distance riders, the Russell seat relies on small built-in springs, rather than foam or a synthetic material, to provide cushioning. The seat is available in either a solo configuration or a two-up version, as seen on this BMW K1100LT.

was not mounted on a touring or sport-touring machine. When I asked him about the suitability of his bike for such events, he chuckled, "It was fine, once I replaced all three 'points of contact:' the seat, the pegs, and the handlebars."

Seats

The seats on many new motorcycles feel great when you sit on them in the showroom, but they become instruments of torture after you've ridden on them for a hundred miles or so. In many cases, it's not a matter of the seat not being soft enough—some seats are too soft to provide adequate support. Even seats that were comfortable at one time become unbearable if the foam becomes compressed from a lot of riding.

A good seat isn't only an issue of comfort; prolonged riding on an inadequate seat can pose potential health risks. Motorcycle police officers, cross-country truckers, and bicyclists often suffer urinary tract infections. Men can also develop a painful inflammation of the prostate as the result of mechanical stress to that area. Replacement or enhancement of a stock seat is probably the single most important motorcycle modification for riding ultra-distances.

The easiest and least costly way to make a seat more comfortable is to add a cushion to an existing seat. Seat pads are more suitable for casual touring, rather than aggressive riding. A

common complaint about seat cushions is that when making turns at high speed, as when riding through mountain twisties, a rider might feel as if the pad is squirming beneath him.

At the high end of seat cushion selections is the AirHawk, which contains a series of independent but interconnected cells that are inflated with air. Designed to distribute pressure more evenly so that blood flow is maintained, this unique technology has been used for more than 25 years in wheelchair cushions and long-term care mattresses. The AirHawk is equipped with

Though usually found on cruiser-style motorcycles, this Honda sport-tourer has been equipped with highway pegs which will permit the rider to stretch his legs to prevent cramping.

loops so you can secure it to your seat with elastic bands or short straps.

Less expensive seat pad options include the Therm-a-Rest Sport Seat, a miniature version of the Therm-a-Rest mattress pad which costs a fraction of the price of the AirHawk cushion. Iron Butt competitors Michael and Caroline McDaniel use gel pads that have been designed to help hospital patients avoid discomfort from putting pressure on sore tissue. Wanner Associates also offers a polymer seat cushion, the "Butt Buffer." Gel pads are available from other manufacturers as well.

Instead of a cushion, some riders use sheepskin covers, which they contend are warm in winter, cool in summer, and provide additional riding comfort. Other riders are enthusiastic about seat covers made of wooden beads similar to the ones used by taxi drivers. Advocates of the beaded covers claim they not only provide good airflow, the massaging action of the beads increases circulation by relieving concentrated pressure points. As the Whitehorse Press Motorcycling Catalog says in its entry for the covers, "Four million cabbies can't be wrong."

Some riders, including such renowned motorcycle world adventurers as Chris Scott and Gregory Frazier, make their own modifications to make their seats more comfortable. In his *Adventure Motorcycling Handbook,* Chris describes a relatively easy method of bringing new life back into a seat with "sagged-out" foam, or for one with foam that is too soft. "First obtain firm foam from an upholsterer," Chris writes. "Then carefully remove the seat covering to expose the part of the seat where your butt normally rests. After cutting out a large block of the original foam, fill the hole with new, firmer foam. Re-staple the seat covering into place."

Greg takes a different approach. "I am better off purchasing a seat cover and foam for a Gold Wing or similar bike, hand-cutting it to fit the stock base on my standard seat and gluing and stapling it to the base."

Aftermarket seats are available for most motorcycles in a variety of styles and colors, often with optional rider and passenger backrests, which many riders find effective in reducing fatigue to their lower back. Aftermarket seats are

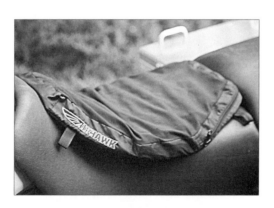

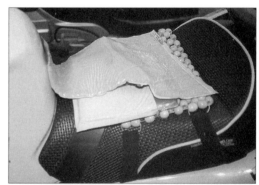

Top left   The AirHawk seat cushion is one way to soothe "cotton butt." These cushions are available from motorcycle dealers in a variety of sizes to fit motorcycles with different size seats.

Top right   The Acton gel pad, originally designed to help bedridden hospital patients, can be found at medical supply stores.

Right   Many riders like the wooden bead seat covering. Larger versions are often used by taxicab drivers.

available from Corbin, Diamond Custom Seats, Mustang, Hartco, Saddlemen, and Sargent.

Among serious long-distance riders, custom seats by Mayer and Russell are considered the most comfortable, even if they are expensive. They may be ordered by mail, but orders must be accompanied by a photograph of the rider (or riders, if ordering a dual seat) mounted on the motorcycle. The picture will be used to help tailor the seat specifically to the rider. Alternately, a ride-in service is available at additional cost. If you make an appointment and arrive in the morning, your custom seat will be ready in the afternoon. You can test the seat and request necessary adjustment and tuning before you return home.

In addition to having extra padding, seats intended for long-distance riding are often wider than stock models, to offer more support to the rider. However, when you put your feet on the ground, this extra width can make a seat feel "taller," something you need to take into account if you are "inseam challenged." If you are ordering a custom saddle, discuss these concerns with your seatmaker; he can usually make modifications that will minimize these effects while still giving you the padding and support you need.

When ordering a custom seat, you'll have to choose between leather and vinyl. There are advantages and disadvantages to each material. Leather is attractive and more comfortable than vinyl, but it requires more care; it must be treated with a conditioner periodically. In addition, rain covers must be used if a leather seat is exposed to prolonged rain, since water can seep through the stitching to the foam below. Vinyl requires less care than leather and it can be subjected to heavy rain without requiring a rain cover, since the seats generally don't have exposed stitching on the top. However, the disadvantage of vinyl is that it becomes very hot and retains heat, a significant disadvantage in hot weather.

Footpegs

Aside from a sore butt, the most likely discomfort you'll encounter when riding ultra-distances will be leg cramps from sitting in the same position for prolonged periods. Collapsible highway pegs can be attached to the engine guard or to the

Bill Newton

Riders earn an Iron Butt SaddleSore 1,000 Certificate for providing evidence of completing a 1,000-mile ride in 24 hours or less. This feat has been recognized throughout the world as the entry-level accomplishment for membership in the IBA. In 1999, Bill Newton rode 30,000 miles in thirty days, completing *thirty* consecutive SaddleSores.

A modest, soft-spoken retired fireman from Huntington Beach, California, Bill has racked up several other endurance-riding accomplishments. He completed the 8/48 Rally in 1996, becoming one of only a handful of riders who can claim to have ridden through the 48 contiguous states in less than ten days. In 1998 he won the Utah 1088 Rally. He has also completed the Three Flags ride, the Four Corners ride, and the Alberta 2000 Endurance Rally.

"Riding consecutive 1,000-mile days isn't as difficult as it sounds," Newt said. "The main thing is scheduling your tire changes and oil changes properly and figuring out how to deal with boredom. The psychological issue of boredom was one of the most overwhelming feelings that I remember from my multiple 1,000-mile per day ride. After a week or so I began to wonder what I was missing out on in the rest of the world. I'm convinced that installation of a satellite radio would be a valuable asset for such long rides. I'm looking into installing one on my motorcycle now." ■

Eric Navratil

Eric Navratil started riding dirt bikes when he was 14 but graduated to "Jughead," a 1993 BMW R80ST, shortly after he turned 16 and received his motorcycle driving license. Soon after, Eric's father, David Navratil, took him to the Waltz Across Texas Rally. Eric caught the long-distance riding bug immediately.

When Eric learned that the youngest rider to complete a SaddleSore 1000 ride had been 17 years old, he became determined to earn a SaddleSore Award before his 17th birthday, a feat he accomplished.

In addition to riding, Eric is an avid musician. He installed an MP3 player on Jughead before he started taking long trips. "I advocate music when riding," Eric says. "I always have something musical running through my head anyway, so it seemed natural to install a CD/MP3 player on my motorcycle. I get more than 100 selections on each disc. I can interchange MP3 discs with regular CDs." ■

front of the frame of the motorcycle to give you a means for stretching your legs and resting your feet during long rides.

There are a few other common tricks for warding off leg cramps. When you're riding solo, you may find it helpful to occasionally put your feet on the passenger pegs for a few minutes during stretches of undemanding road. Or, you could let your legs dangle a bit off the pegs—but beware of road debris that could catch your foot. Depending on how your footpegs are oriented, you may be able to stand up for short stretches as well.

Middle-aged riders who favor sport bikes but whose bodies can't withstand riding in a contorted seating position can use footpeg lowering kits to provide additional legroom, though they will reduce a bike's lean angle, which makes them less popular with aggressive riders.

Handlebars and Grips

After your seat and pegs, your handlebars probably offer the most options for modifying your bike to better suit your individual conformation and riding style. Many riders report the development of sharp pains just below their neck and either between their shoulders, or behind one shoulder or the other. This malady is generally the result of prolonged mechanical stress from the ergonomic positioning of the bike's handlebars. Your local motorcycle dealer may be one of the best resources for test-driving handlebars with differing lengths and characteristics.

If the overall shape of your bars seems okay, but your reach is just a little too long, you might try a set of bar-backs, which move the handlebars closer to the rider to reduce stress on arms and wrists, a problem commonly associated with sport-touring motorcycles that require riders to assume a forward posture.

It's also important to provide your hands with some protection from the elements. Hand guards similar to those found on dual-sport machines will shield your hands from the wind's blast and deflect stones and other flying debris. If you've ever taken a direct hit to your hands from a large stone (or even a large insect), you'll appreciate having hand protectors.

Heated handgrips are a relatively inexpensive factory option on many motorcycles and the additional cost is worth it. It's convenient to flip a switch on the panel and get some heat to your hands, especially when you're riding through the mountains where temperatures drop significantly while crossing a pass, then rise again when descending. If your current motorcycle doesn't have heated handgrips, accessory kits for most motorcycles are available from Hot Grips.

Throttle Aids

Many riders find it convenient to have a means of maintaining speed without exerting pressure on the throttle. A key to remaining comfortable is to avoid fatiguing any part of your body, including your right wrist. A factory installed cruise control feature is the cleanest, and probably most effective method of relieving a tired right hand, but it's an option that is only available on a few models of motorcycles.

Simple mechanical throttle locks can be fitted to most machines, however. These devices provide sufficient resistance to hold the throttle open, yet they can easily be overridden with moderate wrist pressure if necessary. Throttle locks can make adjusting a right-hand zipper or mirror much easier.

Perhaps the simplest and least expensive device for reducing wrist fatigue is a throttle rocker, a plastic flange fitted to the grip onto which you can then rest the palm of your hand. A throttle rocker allows the weight of your hand to do some of the work of operating the throttle, although it doesn't provide the same hands-free operation as cruise control or a throttle lock. If you use a throttle rocker, be sure it's positioned so that it won't get caught in the sleeve of your riding suit and interfere with the safe operation of your machine.

Windshield

There are two considerations in selecting or adjusting the windshield on your motorcycle: protecting your body from fatigue by deflecting the wind, and preventing helmet buffeting. Even when your helmet is entirely in the wind, it's possible to be comfortable on some sport bikes with small windshields, if the screen does a good

The Throttlemeister is a popular brand of throttle lock. Turning the knurled knob exerts light pressure to hold the throttle open, so you can take your hand off the accelerator without shutting down the engine.

Gary Eagan once broke his right arm and wrist and he no longer has a full range of motion. His Ducati has been adapted so he can operate it by pulling a lever rather than twisting the grip.

The hand protectors on this dual-sport motorcycle are an optional accessory that are well worth the small cost, especially if you intend to spend any time riding off the pavement. They also help keep your hands warmer in cold weather.

enough job of deflecting wind from the arms and torso.

On some motorcycles with larger windshields, a rider's helmet remains partially in the wind, resulting in an annoying buffeting. It's sometimes tricky to get a windshield adjusted properly, but it's very important in reducing fatigue. Options are available for most motorcycles, both from motorcycle manufacturers and from aftermarket suppliers.

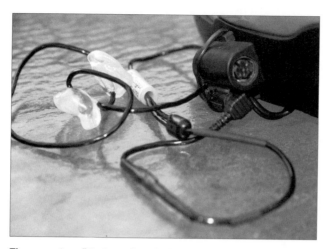

These custom-fitted earplugs include integrated speakers so you can wear them with any helmet.

Many large touring motorcycles have electrically operated windshields that can be adjusted while moving. Once you've used this handy feature, you'll probably never want to do without it.

Sound Systems

Many large touring motorcycles either include a sound system as standard equipment, or offer one as an optional feature. Unless you already have such a motorcycle, the benefits of installing a sound system are controversial, even among long-distance riders. Some riders enjoy the solitude of riding a motorcycle and find anything more than the sound of the motorcycle slicing through the wind an unwelcome intrusion. I know several riders who have removed factory-equipped radios and tape players from their motorcycles, favoring an additional liter or two of storage space over the audio equipment.

Other riders consider a sound system of some type a virtual necessity for long trips. You don't have to install an expensive sound system to enjoy your favorite tunes, however. You could purchase some molded earplugs with integrated speakers and plug into a portable cassette or CD player. This relatively inexpensive solution will kill two birds with one stone: you'll have earplugs and music too. My own experiences with earplug speakers has been very good and I find the sound quality to be incredible. When I'm not listening to music, they function as well as any other earplugs I've tried.

Many riders who tour extensively with a passenger find an intercom system even more important than a radio or cassette or CD player. It's pleasant to be able to comment about the passing scenery or discuss the next pit stop without having to scream over the sound of the wind and engine noise. If your motorcycle doesn't have a fairing that can accommodate the installation of a complete sound system, consider a tankbag sound system that includes an AM/FM radio, cassette tape player, CB radio, or CD player, such as those available from E&E Products ("Tank Tunes") and from Versabag. If you own more than one motorcycle, you can then use the same sound system on all of them.

CHAPTER 2

Safety

Long-distance riding need not be any more dangerous than you're willing to permit it to be. You'll need to both learn your limits and learn how you can expand them safely as you gain experience. The volume of accident-free miles logged each year by riders in the long-distance community is testament to how seriously they take this responsibility. As with all suggestions in this book, adopt only those compatible with your skill and comfort level.

To ride longer distances, you will have to develop skills that only come of experience. Riding at night and in bad weather present their own sets of challenges, as does riding on the interstates—all situations few recreational motorcyclists seek out.

Give yourself every advantage. Be conspicuous and predictable in traffic, using gear that enhances your visibility to other motorists. Establish good habits early and strive to reinforce them as you gain the experience you need to be comfortable and safe under varying conditions.

Minimizing Fatigue

The need for sleep results *primarily* from a need to rest the brain, rather than to rest the body. The brain does not function well indefinitely. It must be "shut down" and permitted to rejuvenate itself. Staying physically fit, however, seems to enable a person to go longer before becoming tired. You'll find that if you maintain an exercise program, eat well, and keep your weight under control, you'll tire less easily than if you're overweight and haven't been exercising.

Since sleep is required primarily to rest the brain, avoiding mental stress seems to delay the onset of fatigue. If you don't permit yourself to fall victim to such minor annoyances as poorly inserted earplugs, insufficient clothing to stay warm and dry, or nearly running out of fuel, you'll be able to ride longer before mental fatigue sets in. If there is anything that aggravates you, consider it carefully. There is usually a solution that will alleviate the problem.

For example, I used to find it difficult to locate the main zipper on my riding suit on the move, especially if I was wearing heavily padded gloves. I solved the problem by attaching a small flashlight to the zipper pull. Not only am I

Don't ignore such a warning—especially after you've recognized one or more of your *own* warning signs.

no longer fumbling for my zipper, I now have a handy source of light for reading maps or searching through my tankbag at night.

Minor annoyances often become major aggravations during a long ride. Instead of tolerating a distraction, you should stop as soon as is safely possible and correct the situation. I often remove my earplugs during a fuel stop, especially if I enter the store to talk to the clerk. If I pull back onto the highway without them, the roar of the wind soon reminds me of my oversight. I always pull onto the shoulder and insert my earplugs before continuing; if I were to continue to ride without them, I'd tire more quickly.

Bob Higdon

Bob Higdon's advice on running the Iron Butt Rally would probably be: "Forget it!"

Bob is well known in the BMW motorcycling community for his role as "Editor at Large" of *On the Level,* the magazine of the BMW Rider's Association, the second-largest BMW motorcycle club in the world. He's also known as the IBA's designated hitter for public relations and legal affairs.

Since 1993, fans of the Iron Butt Rally have eagerly awaited Bob's daily written accounts of rally happenings. In 2001 he participated in the rally as a competitor, leaving responsibility for the daily Internet postings to Iron Butt veteran Warren Harhay.

Bob contends that his first Iron Butt Rally will also be his last. "I hated everything about it," Bob stated at the end of the rally. "It isn't my kind of ride."

During future rallies, Bob may return to his role of scribe, witnessing the agony of the event from the sidelines. ■

It's worth taking an additional moment to ensure that I'm going to be comfortable.

Many riders are reluctant to stop soon after taking off if they are traveling with other riders, as they don't want to delay the group. Stop anyway. Your companions usually will have forgotten the inconvenience by the time the group stops next. If someone questions you about it, apologize for having had to stop and make an effort to ensure you're ready to ride after future stops.

The Importance of Good Habits

Good *habitual* safe riding provides a motorcyclist with a margin of safety. When you've become tired, you're more likely to forget to signal a lane change or to anticipate a left turn from an approaching vehicle—unless the behavior is so ingrained as to be nearly automatic. It may seem like carrying this to an extreme, but I try to discipline myself to signal lane changes when there is no other traffic nearby. I usually stop to wait for a red light to change in the middle of a deserted intersection—even in the wee hours of the morning.

Speed

A prevalent misconception about riders who travel long distances is that high daily mileage is attributable to high speed. Experienced long-distance riders know that high speed isn't a significant factor in packing in a lot of miles, however. As you build mileage, you'll realize that you don't have to ride much faster than you already do. Consistency is a much more important factor. For more on this topic, see Chapter 4: Building Mileage.

Most riders with whom I've traveled stay within the posted speed limit while on secondary streets in populated areas. When on freeways, they ride a little faster than the flow of traffic; it's actually dangerous to ride at or below posted speed limits if traffic is flowing faster than that—especially in some areas of the country. There are some areas in west Texas where you would be at risk if you were only five (or sometimes ten) miles per hour over the speed limit. You'd be run down by an 18-wheeler.

Motorcyclists traveling multi-lane freeways when traffic is heavy should travel in the left lane and ride slightly faster than the flow of traffic. In the slow lane you'll be more likely to be rear-ended by tailgaters or run off the road when vehicles move to the right to exit the freeway. If you stay in the left portion of the leftmost lane, it's easier to see when traffic will be slowing ahead, and there's usually enough room on the left shoulder to make an escape if necessary.

Tailgating

Riders sometimes become impatient with drivers who remain in the left lane when they aren't passing. I've seen riders impatiently flash their high beams and ride the vehicle's bumper to intimidate them into moving to the right. I've also witnessed cases in which a driver has permitted the motorcycle to pass, only to repay the rider by riding *his* tail.

Don't intentionally antagonize a potentially unbalanced or intoxicated driver who is commanding a vehicle weighing four or five times as much as yours. Riding aggressively is not only dangerous and stressful, but it contributes to the

A small flashlight not only can be an easy-to-find "handle" for locating a zipper pull, it also provides a light source. Attaching something like this to a main zipper makes it easier to adjust your ventilation while on the move. A long section of leather shoelace can be fashioned into a sturdy zipper pull.

Dr. Gregory Frazier

Dr. Gregory Frazier is the only American to have circumnavigated the globe by motorcycle four times. His travels have taken him over a million miles and he has literally ridden a motorcycle to the ends of the earth: Deadhorse, Alaska; Ushuaia, Argentina; North Cape, Norway; Cape Agulhaus, South Africa; and Bluff, New Zealand.

Frazier has written numerous books on the subject of motorcycling, including many works that focus on off-highway travel such as *BMW GSing Around the World, Riding South: Mexico, Central America and South America by Motorcycle,* and *Alaska by Motorcycle.* He has, on occasion, sponsored off-highway rallies and events.

Greg has some strong feelings about the role speed should play in long-distance touring.

"What I have learned over the years about the game of adventuring around the globe on two wheels and long rides came from my experience as a street rider, crashing as the result of speed and youthful foolishness, which eventually got me into professional road racing," Greg says. "My equation is Speed = Pain; it is just a function of Time. Put another way, I have learned it is not how fast we ride through life, but how long we do it."

When not adventuring around the world, Frazier, a native American who takes the name "Sun Chaser," lives in the Big Horn Mountains of Montana on the Crow Indian Reservation. Additional information is available on his web site at www.horizonsunlimited.com/gregfrazier. ∎

Mary Sue Luetschwager

In 1995 Suzy Luetschwager (then Suzy Johnson) entered Iron Butt Rally history when she became the first woman to complete the rally on a Harley-Davidson, the "Iron Butter-fly." The following year the beloved Harley was stolen from a motel parking lot near Denver, two days before the start of the 8/48 Rally. Suzy purchased a gently-used BMW motorcycle and finished the 48-state rally in third place. In the 1997 Iron Butt, Suzy rode the BMW to an impressive sixth-place finish, ahead of more than 70 other competitors.

Spending long hours on the nation's highways wasn't new to Suzy when she became interested in motorcycling in the early '90s. Suzy is a long-haul driver for Roadway Express, specializing in driving 18-wheelers with dual trailers from one end of the country to the other. Not only does she drive the big rigs—she competes in truck-driving rodeos in which she matches her skills at handling the enormous trucks against the skills of drivers from around the country. In 2001, she was State Grand Champion and first in the twin trailer division. Suzy is also a member of a Roadway Express team that visits schools and fairs to promote safety.

She often cautions her motorcyclist friends to avoid the "No Zone" behind big trucks. "Tailgating a truck irritates the driver, and is *very* dangerous," she maintains. "Although truckers check their tires regularly, they have no control over what may be on the pavement that can cause a blowout. I have seen a blowout knock clearance lights off the truck and break off mud flaps. I shudder to think of the consequences that could befall a rider struck by such a large flying object. Stay away from big trucks!" ∎

negative perception that some motorists have about motorcyclists.

Tailgating also deprives you of a good view of the road ahead of you, so you'll be less likely to spot hazardous road debris in time to react safely. It can be an especially dangerous practice during bad weather or when you're likely to encounter animals.

Big Trucks

Tailgating any vehicle is a bad idea, but doing it behind an 18-wheeler is especially dangerous. Your field of view is more limited than when following an automobile and there's the added danger of being struck by flying debris if the truck should have a blowout.

No one knows more about the danger of tailgating big trucks than Iron Butt veteran and Roadway Express driver Suzy Luetschwager. "A blowout can blast off the truck's heavy mudflap with the force of a bowling ball going 60 mph," Suzy says. "Another danger is that drivers don't like it when a vehicle is following them too closely. Instead of paying attention to the road, the driver will begin worrying about the vehicle that's on their tail."

Mirrors

Adequate mirrors are needed to operate your motorcycle safely. Selecting and adjusting your mirrors to completely eliminate blind spots will also allow you to avoid redundant head checks. Not only will you be able to keep your eyes on the road in front of you, you can eliminate some of the wasted movement of turning your head to look over your shoulder several hundred times per day. Remember that a key to increasing comfort and decreasing the onset of fatigue is to minimize the amount of energy you expend on unnecessary repetitive movements, no matter how small they may seem. Additional mirrors are available at most automobile parts stores, as are small, wide-angle mirrored inserts with which you can augment your existing mirrors.

You must develop a system for quickly readjusting your mirrors if they are moved, as when the motorcycle is washed or the mirrors have been cleaned. While riding in the right lane of a four-lane highway, shift your eyes to look in your left mirror. There should *never* be a moment when a vehicle approaching from the rear isn't visible. First, the vehicle will appear in the left mirror. As the vehicle passes, but before its image leaves the left mirror, it should be visible in the wide-angle insert. Before the image disappears from the insert, it should appear in your peripheral vision as you continue to look straight ahead.

Next, ride in the left lane and observe your right mirror while keeping your head pointed straight ahead. As you pass a vehicle, its image should appear in your wide-angle insert before the vehicle disappears from your peripheral vision. Before the image disappears from the insert, it should become visible in the mirror and should remain visible until you are well past the vehicle.

After both mirrors have been adjusted to eliminate blind spots, park your motorcycle and observe, from a sitting position, how the mirrors are adjusted. When the mirror on my motorcycle is adjusted properly, I can see about half of my arms in the reflection, and the top of the mirror is aligned with the top of my shoulder. Of course, you will have different points of reference, but the idea is to be able to readjust your mirrors quickly and easily when you need to.

Be Reflective

To be more conspicuous to other motorists, wear something reflective. If you have leathers or a riding suit that has little or no reflective material, wear a reflective vest or use extra reflective tape on the backs of your saddlebags. Black reflective tape is especially effective for increasing your conspicuity. By day, the tape appears black, but when exposed to vehicle headlights at night, it glows very brightly. I purchased a roll of the stuff from Galls, but it's available from some automobile supply stores too.

Perhaps the ultimate accouterment in visibility is the Aerostich Roadcrafter or Darien jacket in Hi-Viz Lime Yellow. The color carries much more visual punch than any other color. A friend who purchased one told me he felt confident that no motorist could possibly claim that he didn't see him. On the other hand, he feared that some

These wide-angle inserts are inexpensive and sold in most auto accessory stores. When they have been adjusted properly, you can eliminate blind spots.

Will Lee's rally-equipped Harley-Davidson with additional rear-view capabilities also sports a BCI auxiliary fuel cell from Summit Racing, GPS receiver, and integrated radar and CB radio.

motorists might consider it their civic duty to run over anyone wearing such an obnoxious color.

Lights

The motorcycle's lights serve three important functions: to illuminate the road after dark, to

Black reflective tape isn't visible during the daylight, but when a vehicle's lights shine on it after dark, it becomes very noticeable. The tape is especially useful if your riding suit doesn't have much reflective material.

make the motorcycle more conspicuous to other motorists, and to permit you to see accessory controls at night. For the last problem, note that on some motorcycles, accessory switches can be swapped out for illuminated ones. Many riders add small gooseneck-style lamps as well. The most popular of these is the Littlite, which is seen on a high percentage of endurance-equipped motorcycles.

If you're planning to ride throughout the night, especially where wildlife is present, con-

sider investing in a High Intensity Discharge (HID) lighting system. This is the single most important investment that you can make to increase your margin of safety at night. HID headlamps utilize xenon gas light sources rather than a traditional filament bulb. An HID system includes a ballast and an igniter for each lamp. A high-voltage charge from the igniter causes an arc to light between the electrodes of the xenon gas light source; the "white" light that is produced provides better illumination for all-weather driving, enabling the rider to see more clearly. HID lights produce up to three times more illumination than incandescent lights, while using less power. HID lights also provide a "life of vehicle" light source, so you never have to replace burned-out bulbs.

Baja Designs offers kits that permit motorcyclists to convert their headlights to HID technology. HID driving lights are available from several companies, including PIAA and Hella.

Driving Lights

Many riders who travel extensively at night install high-powered driving lights and have them wired with a separate switch so that whenever the switch is in the ON position, the driving lights come on when the high beam is activated. When aimed high and wide to illuminate the sides of the road, beyond the reach of the headlight's high beam, they provide advance warning of animals that are near the road. Driving lights are

The Hurt Report

The Hurt Report is available through The National Technical Information Service, Springfield, Virginia 22161. The specific report that must be requested is:

Motorcycle Accident Cause Factors and Identification of Countermeasures
Volume 1: Technical Report, Hurt, H.H., Ouellet, J.V. and Thom, D.R.
Traffic Safety Center
University of Southern California
Los Angeles, California 90007
Contract No. DOT HS-5-01160
January 1981 (Final Report) ∎

very effective in the wide expanses in the west, Canada, and Alaska or in any heavily forested area where the potential appearance of deer, moose, elk, bear, and other wildlife is most worrisome. In more populated areas, the lights must usually be dimmed to avoid blinding other drivers.

Auxiliary driving lights aren't just effective at night. According to the Hurt Report, 75 percent of motorcycle accidents involve collision with other vehicles. The predominant cause is failure of motorists to recognize motorcycles. The addition of auxiliary lights for daytime use can help to make you more conspicuous. Auxiliary lights are available from a variety of manufacturers, such as Motolight, whose halogen units can be mounted on the outside of any motorcycle's fork sliders.

Several years ago, a driver exited a shopping center parking lot in broad daylight and pulled directly into my path. I was able to brake quickly enough to avoid a collision, but the incident startled me. I remember thinking about how infrequently that had happened to me.

An hour or so later at an intersection, another car made an abrupt left turn in front of me. I braked rapidly and avoided an accident, but this incident was a closer call than the first one. As I pulled over to regain my composure, I wondered about the coincidence of two such episodes occurring in such a short period. Then I noticed that, sure enough, my headlight bulb had burned out. The incident reinforced my belief that riders who intentionally ride without their headlights on during the day are foolish. I check my headlight more frequently now and I've added auxiliary lights to my motorcycles.

Modulators

Modulating units, which cause a headlight to quickly flash between high and low beams, attract the attention of other motorists, but I don't recommend them. They are illegal in some states. Modulators can be annoying to motorists, especially if the unit is on while you follow other vehicles. If a rider is courteous enough to switch the modulator off when following other vehicles closely, he may not remember to turn it on again and the unit may not be working when it's

John Harrison equipped his BMW K1200LT with HID lights in preparation for the 2001 Iron Butt Rally. These large PIAA Pro80XT each produces 350,000 candle power. The small driving lights are PIAA 1100X models and the fog lights are PIAA 1400 Ion.

This BMW R1150GS incorporates high-intensity, long-range driving lights (top) and fog lamps (below). The fog lights can be illuminated during the day to provide additional conspicuity to other motorists. The metal integrated headlight protector and oil cooler grille helps prevent damage while riding off-highway.

Russ Downing's rally-equipped Polaris motorcycle sports distinctive Hella Rallye 4000 FF HID driving lights which can just about turn night into day. Russ also found a convenient place to store some additional luggage.

needed. Perhaps most importantly, modulators cannot be used in conjunction with HID lighting systems, which I believe are essential for riding after dark. Auxiliary lights will provide both additional conspicuity *and* additional lighting, without annoying other motorists.

Hyper-Lites

Hyper-Lites are designed to draw additional attention to a motorcycle's taillight when the rider

When you see dead deer on or beside the road, be especially alert for others. Notice that this deer was killed in a heavily populated commercial area. It isn't always necessary to leave civilization to encounter deer and other animals in the road.

is applying the brakes. If you continue to keep pressure on the brakes while you're at a stop sign, the Hyper-Lites will also continue to flash brightly and possibly even prevent your being rear-ended.

Dodging Deer

The Insurance Information Institute claims that every year there are about 750,000 collisions between motorists and deer. The National Safety Council estimates that more than 350,000 deer are killed annually in vehicle accidents. Although these statistics don't differentiate between motorcycles and other vehicles, for riders who travel through sparsely populated rural areas, the risk of hitting wildlife is a serious danger.

The only thing about deer behavior that you can count on is that it will be aberrant. If deer are present, they are likely to dart suddenly into the road. If they are standing in the road, and you attempt to avoid them by swerving around them, they may bolt into your path. Deer seem to be startled into flight by proximity more than anything else. If you see them grazing beside the road, they may look up as you approach, then continue feeding. As you get closer, they are likely to dash in any direction.

If you're going to travel extensively at night, especially in areas with a lot of wildlife, you should augment your headlight with long-range driving lights to give you some advanced warning of animals near the edges of the road.

Detection

Although you may encounter deer in every state at any time of the year, they are more active during the last three months of the year, as they travel more frequently during the fall breeding period. The presence of hunters in the woods each autumn also causes deer to flee. As crops are harvested in the fall and vegetation dies out, deer become more wide-ranging and active in pursuit of food. The grass beside the nation's highways becomes increasingly appealing.

Deer can be out at any time of day, but you are more likely to see them at dusk and dawn. Most clashes with deer occur between 6:30 a.m. and 7:30 a.m. and between 4:30 p.m. and 6:30 p.m. If you travel extensively in rural areas at night, invest in a good set of high-intensity driving lights. Direct the lights so they illuminate the shoulders of the road. As you scan the shoulders, be alert for the reflection of the light in their eyes.

Deer usually travel in groups. If you see a deer cross the road ahead of you, assume that there are others in the vicinity. State highway departments place deer crossing signs where there have been recurrent accidents or frequent sightings of deer in the road, and you should be especially careful when you see them. A deer carcass alongside the road or other evidence of a strike, like fresh red splotches streaked across the highway should also put you on alert.

You'll sometimes see high fences along the shoulders of interstate highways, set back from the road. These are meant to prevent deer from entering the highway, but be careful when the fence ends, as deer will sometimes go around the fence to cross the road.

Evasion

The safest way to avoid striking deer is to ride at or below the speed limit and to remain especially vigilant while riding through deer-infested areas. By reducing your speed and preparing to brake you'll have more time to react to a sudden appearance. If you do strike a deer, you'll probably fare a lot better if you've been able to significantly reduce your speed. Since you'll want to be prepared to brake hard, this would be an especially bad time to be riding in front of a tailgater.

One of the difficulties of touring in Canada and many areas of the northwest United States is the spectacular scenery that can distract riders from focusing on potential wildlife hazards. Although hitting a deer is a very serious concern, hitting a moose, which is much larger, can be even more serious.

Now for the tough part: if you're suddenly surprised by a deer that has darted into your path, is it better to take your chances hitting it, or to swerve and possibly lose control of the motorcycle or collide with oncoming traffic? Swerving is a sufficiently dangerous maneuver that most safety authorities recommend that automobile drivers take their chances hitting the animal, rather than swerve and potentially lose control of the vehicle.

If you decide to swerve, how will you know in which direction to swerve, since a deer's actions can be so unpredictable? Its first leap will be in whatever direction it's facing, but it can then zigzag back into your path. In most circumstances, the best alternative is hard braking in a straight line. That's why it's important to reduce your speed and be prepared to brake before you have to.

I had an accident with a deer while my wife and I were traveling near Edmonton at about sixty miles per hour. The animal suddenly darted into the road from heavy brush and I had no warning. It was the middle of the afternoon in June, not dawn or dusk in the fall. The deer

These DEER CROSSING signs on Interstate 5 in Oregon warn motorists that the state has erected high fences along the highway to funnel deer across the road at these designated crosswalks.

Collisions with wildlife is as serious a problem in Canada as it is in the United States. On this section of highway in British Columbia, the government is conducting a test to determine if they can discourage deer from crossing the highway at night when vehicles are present. A series of reflectors have been placed along the shoulder to deflect the light from vehicle headlights into the woods and field beside the road.

seemed to be traveling alone and there were no DEER CROSSING signs in the area.

Upon impact, the motorcycle began to wobble and lose stability. I opened the throttle all the way and may have also downshifted. I was able to pull safely to the shoulder of the road without dropping the bike. We later confirmed that the deer had been killed. The motorcycle's fairing was damaged and the radiator was slowly leaking coolant, but I was able to ride the motorcycle into Edmonton. I believe that if I had been startled into an evasive swerve, the outcome could have been worse.

Deer Whistles

There's a lot of controversy about whether deer whistles work. Manufacturers of the whistles cite studies suggesting that they work, while their critics cite studies that indicate that deer can't hear them. Even if a deer can hear them, what exactly is it supposed to do about it? And since *you* can't hear the whistles, how will you know they haven't become clogged with dead insects or with dirt and are no longer functioning?

I suspect that whistles don't work, but I use them anyway. They aren't very expensive and are probably as effective as a Saint Christopher medal or a rabbit's foot. Besides, I've only had one collision with a deer and the accident occurred at about the only time since I began riding that I didn't have deer whistles on the motorcycle. Call me superstitious.

Weather

If a rider exercises common sense and both he and his machine are properly prepared for it, it's possible to continue riding in heavy rain in relative safety and comfort. Of course, it would be foolish to continue if your clothing doesn't keep you dry and warm or if you're riding on worn tires without sufficient tread. ABS braking systems, which are becoming more popular on touring motorcycles, can give you an additional measure of control when roads are wet.

Riding in heavy weather is like riding at night—a rider cannot see or be seen as clearly as in daylight. Motorists who don't slow during rain compound the problem. Expect to encounter more incidents of sudden lane changes and erratic behavior by motorists during bad weather. Slow down! Experienced riders scrub speed during the rain, even when they are dressed properly and safely equipped for such conditions.

Thunderstorms

It's very dangerous to continue to ride a motorcycle during lightning storms. As motorcycle columnist and *Proficient Motorcyclist* author

David Hough has observed, "Rubber tires won't insulate you from a lightning strike, and your head makes a pretty good lightning rod. The odds aren't good riding into a thunderstorm." Having to backtrack is often disappointing, but sometimes it's smarter than continuing to ride into deteriorating conditions.

The good news is that thunderstorms are often localized and usually pass in a half-hour or so. Rain can go on all day, but heavy thunder and lightning usually don't last long. Whenever you hear thunder nearby or see lightning flashes within a few miles, head for cover. When using an overpass for shelter, park your machine as far from the roadway as possible, activate hazard-warning lights, and move away from the motorcycle. If you're lucky, you'll find a self-service car wash where you can park the motorcycle and wait for the storm to pass.

Hail

Hailstorms are often accompanied by very strong winds, including tornadoes. Like thunderstorms, hailstorms usually pass within a half-hour or so.

I once found myself in a heavy hailstorm on a desolate stretch of highway between Augusta and Wolf Creek, Montana. As soon as large hailstones began pelting me, I tried to return to Augusta. The wind became so strong and the visibility so poor that I was concerned about being able to keep the motorcycle on the road. I parked on the shoulder, walked to a drainage ditch beside the road, and placed myself as low into the ditch as I could without entering the water. Within 15 minutes or so, the storm had passed and the sun was shining.

Snow and Ice

As dangerous as it is to ride in lightning or hail, riding during icy conditions is even worse. Although few riders deliberately travel into areas where icy conditions are expected, motorcyclists who ride 365 days per year sometimes find themselves riding in snow and ice—even in Texas. Short of parking the motorcycle and sending for a trailer or pickup truck (sometimes the only sensible option), it can sometimes be better to continue on rather than turn back. Depending on the storm's direction of travel, conditions behind you may have deteriorated even more than those ahead.

When snow and freezing conditions begin, it's advisable to ride in the tracks of other vehicles. Study the spray being kicked up by the tires of the vehicles in front of you; as long as the spray is visible, the road isn't frozen yet. When spray is no longer visible, it's time to pull onto the shoulder and stop riding. The reflection of lights on the road will also give you a clue about how frozen the surface is. When the reflections go from being very sharp to being blurry, you're on ice. Pay attention to your temperature gauge;

it will also give you some warning that freezing is about to occur.

Trying to ride on ice is almost certainly going to put the most experienced riders down, and other vehicles will be unlikely to stop for you. If it's necessary to ride in icy conditions until a safe haven is found, ride slowly on the shoulder of the road with hazard lights blinking. The shoulder, where gravel, stones, and other debris have accumulated, will usually provide more traction—at least for a while.

Tires

Proper tire selection, care, and repair are much more critical to the motorcyclist than to other motorists. For motorcyclists, tires are a key element in staying upright. Proper inflation is one of the most important factors for both safety and tire life. Overinflated tires will give you a harsh ride and will wear out quickly. Underinflation can be even more critical, however, as it can greatly reduce the life of a tire, as well as cause poor handling, especially when cornering. Tire pressures should be measured when your tires are cold. Check your tire pressure daily when you're on a long trip.

Many riders are so cautious about ensuring that their tires are always inflated properly that they have installed the Kisan Technologies Tire Alert System. The unit provides a small readout on the instrument panel that provides an accurate reading of tire pressure at all times. An added benefit of the system is that riders are alerted in advance of a flat, assuming the flat is caused by a slow leak.

Tires are sometimes damaged without going flat immediately. Inspect them periodically to determine whether they have picked up a nail or have received any deep slashes that could cause the tire to fail.

There are many ways to equip your motorcycle with a thermometer. This rider attached a temperature strip to the top lip of his windshield.

Selection

Motorcycle tire manufacturers have web sites that list the models of motorcycle their tires will fit. It's risky to change tire sizes unless a representative of the motorcycle manufacturer or a qualified dealer has approved the proposed change, as a different size tire will affect the steering geometry of the motorcycle. Tire manufacturers work closely with motorcycle manufacturers to ensure that proper tires are used with various models of motorcycles.

Motorcycle tires are intended to be run in sets, and mixing them may result in tires that aren't compatible in terms of tread patterns, composition, and handling characteristics. It's especially dangerous to mix a bias-ply tire with a radial tire. Before you violate any rules, be certain to consult someone with sufficient tire expertise.

No matter which tire you select, your choice will be a compromise. You can select a high-performance, sport-oriented tire that provides maximum grip but wears out quickly. Or, you can select a high-mileage tire, but you won't be able to push the motorcycle through the twisties as

The road looks clear, but this is the time to remain vigilant for patches of ice obscured by shadows. "Black" ice, which is invisible to a rider, is especially dangerous.

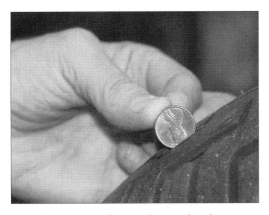

If you don't have a tire tread gauge handy, you can use a Lincoln penny. If the tread barely touches Abe's head, it's time to replace the tire.

Bill Thweatt admits that he can never seem to remember how much pressure he's supposed to use for his tires, so he affixed some stick-on numerals to his windshield as a reminder.

aggressively as you could with the softer tires. A standard tire will be somewhere in-between.

I put a lot of miles on my motorcycles and I don't like the inconvenience of having to make frequent trips to the motorcycle shop for new tires. I always choose the highest mileage tire available, since I don't ride so aggressively that I've ever felt unsafe or uncomfortable with this option.

Most of my friends in the long-distance community favor high-mileage tires. I've used Dunlop 491s on my K1100LTs and typically get about 15,000 miles from the rear tire. This is also the tire of choice for the Honda Gold Wing models 1200 and 1500, with riders getting up to 20,000 miles from the rear tire and more than 30,000 from the front. Michelin Macadam 100X tires provide about 15,000 miles of riding on the BMW R1100/1150RT. Dunlop 205s provide almost the same mileage. Dunlop 402s seem to provide about the same mileage on Harley-Davidsons.

Because major tire manufacturers discontinue some tire models and introduce others frequently, it's best to solicit thoughts from other long-distance riders for the latest opinions on high-mileage tires. LDRider is the best source of information, as are other Internet lists and bike specific lists, such as Internet BMW Riders.

Some riders go through tires so frequently, and the expense represents such a high percent-

age of their riding budget, that they acquire equipment to mount and balance tires themselves. Tires can be purchased via mail order or over the Internet at significant savings over dealer prices. Although the air compressor and mounting and balancing equipment can run to more than a thousand dollars, it doesn't take long to recover the cost of mounting tires several times per year. As a side benefit, these riders don't have to schedule visits to the dealer for tire changes.

Avoiding Punctures

It won't be possible to avoid punctures altogether, but there are some tricks to minimize them.

When you're riding alone or when you're the first rider in a group, select a riding position to the left of the center of the lane, approximately in the left wheel track of four-wheeled vehicles. This position will place you in a section of the lane that has usually been swept clean of screws which have worked their way loose from vehicles (a major cause of punctures), and of other debris. When you're behind a rider who is using the left wheel track, use the right wheel track, just a little to the right of the center of the lane. As with the left wheel track, this area has been swept clean by passing motorists. You'll also be following proper group riding practice by riding staggered from the rider in front of you.

The area of the lane where you are *most* likely to suffer a puncture is the center of the lane, where debris collects. You shouldn't ride directly in the center of the lane anyway. If you're entering a right-hand sweeper, you can see oncoming traffic sooner if you're near the centerline, and if you're entering a left-hand sweeper, you'll see more if you're in the right portion of the lane.

Once the debris makes it to the shoulder, it stays there. If you've walked along the side of the road, you've probably observed all manner of stuff that could contribute to a puncture. Keep an eye out for such things if you have to pull off the road. Along with screws and nails, you could find dislodged mufflers, sections of tail pipe, and "alligators" (those strips of tire tread shed by trucks when they experience a blowout). The longer such debris has been on the roadway, the more likely it is that traffic has swept it to the center of the lane or to the shoulder.

The potential sudden appearance of large pieces of debris in the road is another reason to avoid tailgating. You'll appreciate a few seconds warning if you're going to have to avoid a large piece of rubbish.

If you venture off-highway and travel unpaved roads, you'll sometimes face an additional problem: sharp rocks. Although you can't avoid the possibility of a flat altogether, having fresh tires can help. As tires wear thin, they are much more susceptible to being punctured than if they have deep tread.

Internal sealants are designed to be injected into a motorcycle's tires to instantly seal small punctures as soon as they occur. While you ride, a protective layer of the sealant coats the inner surface of your tire. If your tire is punctured, the centrifugal force of the rotating tire and the internal air pressure force the sealant into the hole. The tire literally fixes itself. Since what would otherwise be a slow leak is stopped as soon as it starts, proper tire pressure is maintained. A typical internal sealant of this variety is the Ride-On Tire Protection System by Inovex Industries.

Repair.   Repairing and inflating a tire is not difficult provided you have the proper tools and some practice using them. If you've never repaired a puncture, practice by intentionally puncturing and repairing an old tire. Perform the exercise in the parking lot of a motorcycle shop, using tires you're about to replace.

Except for off-road and vintage motorcycles, most modern motorcycles, including those with spoked wheels, use tubeless tires. The Stop and Go Tire Plugger is a little heavier and takes up more room than a basic kit, but it's more effective for repairing tubeless tires, as the mushroom-headed tire plugs will seat themselves on the inner wall of the tire; conventional plugs are not anchored to the inner wall and must rely on glue to hold them in place within the tread.

More traditional tire repair kits typically contain an auguring tool for cleaning and roughening the puncture, glue, plugs, CO_2 cartridges, and a screw-on inflation valve. These kits can be effective for repairing a puncture, but they are usually a one-shot operation. Although several plugs are provided, I've often wasted several before I got one seated exactly right, and several CO_2 cartridges are needed to inflate the tire, so if the fix doesn't take on the first try, you'll proba-

The Stop & Go Tire Plugger is one of the most popular tire repair kits used by long-distance riders. The plug gun inserts a small rubber plug into the tread of a punctured tire, and the mushroom head of the plug prevents it from being dislodged. The messy glues needed to make other types of plugs adhere to the inside wall of the tread are not needed. The kit is very compact and easily fits into the bottom of one of your luggage bags. (courtesy of Stop & Go)

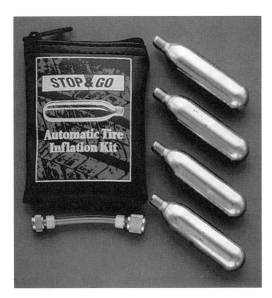

By combining a tire inflation kit, such as this model from Stop & Go, with a good tire repair kit, you'll have everything you need to repair a flat and fill the tire with enough air to get you to an air pump. (courtesy of Stop & Go)

bly be out of luck. If you are going to be riding in remote places, be sure to carry extra air cartridges.

Repairing a puncture in a tube-type tire is usually more complicated and challenging than repairing a tubeless tire. The former entails removing the wheel from the motorcycle, breaking the bead, removing the tube from the tire, repairing the tube and tire, replacing the wheel, and getting the repaired tire and tube to seat properly. Many motorcycle dealers, motorcycle supply stores, and automobile supply stores offer tire irons and the other tools needed to repair tube-type tires.

Inflation. After repairing a tire of any type, it must be filled with air. CO_2 cartridges don't take up much space and they fill a tire quickly; three cartridges are required to inflate a tire, and I usually carry at least a half-dozen of them. The Ultraflate Tire Inflator, an inexpensive, compact device that can accommodate both threaded and unthreaded cartridges, is an improvement over the flimsy plastic inflation valves often supplied with repair kits.

Some motorcycle shops and mail order houses market the Engineair Power Pump, which uses a motorcycle's engine as an air compressor to inflate tires via a hose that screws into a sparkplug hole; the unit will inflate a tire in about one minute.

A small air compressor powered by the motorcycle's electrical system can be especially handy when you are heading out off pavement, as it is often necessary to deflate and inflate tires when traversing long stretches of sand or loose footing. The Airman AM654 portable air compressor, available from PerformanceBike and other Internet retailers, comes recommended, but it can take more than 15 minutes to inflate a flat tire. BestRest Products, which caters to the dual-sport community, offers an even more compact unit.

The simplest, but probably least effective means of temporarily repairing a puncture is to inflate the tire with a latex-like substance from an aerosol can, which inflates the tire to a moderate pressure. The product is popular enough with motorists that you can usually find it at auto parts shops as well as convenience stores. These cans don't work on large holes, but may get you to a garage where a proper repair can be made. Dunlop recommends that you not use these types of sealants as they may adversely affect ply material and mask secondary damage caused by a penetrating object. They contend that reliance upon sealants can result in sudden tire failure and accident.

Replacement

Excessively worn tires are more likely to get punctured and they are dangerous on wet pavement. A tread with sufficient depth provides a channel for water to escape so that the tire retains adequate contact with the pavement. Absent this escape channel, water will stay between the tire and the pavement to cause a situation known as "hydroplaning." You'll lose control of the motorcycle if the tire is suspended on a cushion of water.

Tires should be removed from service before they reach the tread wear indicator bars, or when 1/32 of an inch of tread pattern depth remains. I carry a tread-depth gauge in my tankbag and check tread depth periodically. If you don't have a gauge, use a U.S. Lincoln penny; when a coin inserted into the tire shows that the tread barely touches the top of Abe's head, it's time to replace the tires.

Some riders insist that for safety reasons you replace a punctured tire as soon as you can, but some tire manufacturers acknowledge that some punctures can safely be repaired. Dunlop recommends only permanent plug-patch repairs of small (maximum 1/4-inch diameter) tread area punctures from within the dismounted tire by a qualified tire repair shop or motorcycle dealer. They recommend against performing an exterior repair or using an inner tube as a substitute for a proper repair. They also insist that no form of temporary repair should be attempted because secondary damage caused by a penetrating ob-

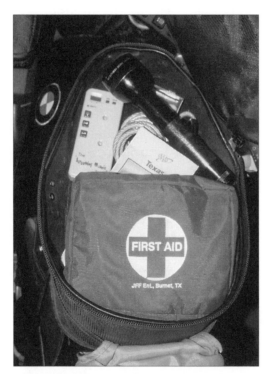

The JFF first-aid kit was designed with the motorcyclist in mind and it comes highly recommended from *Motorcycle Consumer News* and several other leading motorcycle journals. It can be conveniently packed in the top of a tankbag within easy reach, and it has everything you might need to handle most mishaps you are likely to encounter, including items for back pain, insect bites, upset stomach, and headache, in addition to a good assortment of bandages and first-aid creams.

ject may not be detected and tire or tube deflation may occur later.

Tool Kit

The amount of space dedicated to a tool kit should depend on the reliability of the motorcycle and the mechanical skill of the rider. Except for a pair of vice grips, a flashlight, duct tape, and some zip-tie fasteners, I've generally packed little more than the tools provided by the bike's manufacturer. Some riders carry enough tools to dismantle and rebuild their engine beside the road. With my limited mechanical experience, the additional tools would just take up precious luggage space and reduce my carrying capacity. This makes mechanically adept friends shudder, but I've never carried more tools than I feel I'm competent to use. I've made minor roadside repairs from time to time and found the standard tool set to be adequate. Rather than rely on a complete set of tools and my limited mechanical expertise, I ride motorcycles that are serviced regularly and which my local dealer keeps in good repair.

One critical addition to any rider's tool kit is a roll of duct tape. It's probably the single most important enhancement that you can make to your collection of tools and emergency supplies.

First-Aid Kit

The advisability of packing a first-aid kit should be obvious. The challenge is to acquire one that contains sufficient materials to be useful in case of an accident without taking up too much storage space.

Although you could probably save a few dollars by purchasing items separately and assembling your own kit, it's more convenient to purchase one that includes the necessary items. JFF Enterprises sells a clearly marked first-aid kit that has been recommended by the IBA and it's small enough to fit in your tankbag without monopolizing the entire space.

Some riders carry aspirin or other pain relievers for use when muscles become sore. Most pain relievers, including aspirin, have the unwelcome side effect of inducing drowsiness. Many pain relievers are also blood-thinners, and you may wish to retain your blood's natural clotting ability in case of an accident.

Cell Phones

Cell phones have become prevalent as convenience items, but they can also give you a measure of safety during an emergency. Today's most advanced cell phones include integrated Palm organizers, which provide a means of incorporating both devices into a compact package.

If you install an audio headset in your helmet, you can connect it to your cell phone with a device that permits you to place or receive cellular telephone calls while riding. The unit provides the same luxury enjoyed by motorists with "hands-free" cell phones. Your cell phone can be set to answer automatically, so you don't have to touch the phone to receive a call while moving. Before leaving home, also ensure that your phone has been programmed for "one touch dialing" so you won't be distracted when making a call on the move.

The Kennedy Technology Group markets the electronic apparatus needed to integrate a cell phone, CB radio, and radar detector with a standard motorcycle helmet headset.

Although I've used a cell phone headset device, I find talking on the phone while riding to be sufficiently distracting that I typically pull off the highway to take or place a call. I sometimes use speed dial to make a connection while moving, then pull over when I'm sure the call has been answered. Even though I stop, being able to use the phone without dismounting or removing my helmet is a great convenience.

If you plan to use a cell phone extensively while traveling, look closely at the roaming charges associated with the calling plan you sign up for. If you don't have a cell phone, it's a good idea to get a calling card or prepaid phone card before you take a long trip. They can save you the trouble of carrying enough coins to make a long-distance call.

Trust Your Instincts

One of the most interesting observations that I've made about ardent long-distance riders is the amount of respect that they afford their in-

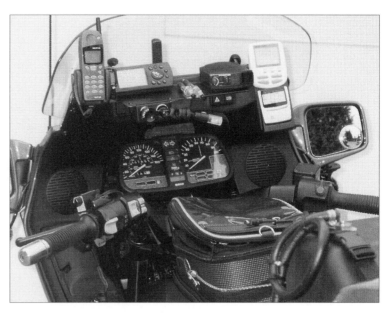

Pete Sutherland mounted his cell phone in the cockpit of his BMW, beside the GPS receiver, radar detector, and dual timers.

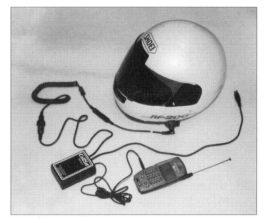

Hooking up a cellular phone with the Kennedy Cell Set is very easy: one wire into the cellular phone, one end into the helmet headset, and the last wire plugs into the motorcycle's audio system jack.

stincts, or "sixth sense." Gary Eagan, unquestionably one of the most experienced riders in the endurance community, was the first I heard comment about how respectful he was whenever the hair on the back of his neck tingled, causing him to feel apprehensive. On one occasion when Gary didn't show up for a planned endurance ride, he acknowledged that he just didn't feel comfortable about participating in that particular rally.

When I asked Carolyn McDaniel about her experience riding the Iron Butt Rally two-up with her husband Michael on their Ducati, she made an interesting comment: "It helps to com-

In the heat of competition, two-up riders Michael and Carolyn McDaniel have learned to trust one another and function as a true team. They enjoyed the 1999 Iron Butt Rally so much that they returned to do it again in 2001.

pletely trust each other. On the '99 Iron Butt when bonus packets were handed out for the Washington to Maine leg, the points clearly indicated we should route ourselves through Plano, Texas. We mapped out our leg and were getting ready to head that way when Michael said, 'I just get a bad feeling about heading down there. I don't think we should do it.' My unhesitating response was, 'Then we won't.' "

Carolyn told me about a similar incident that occurred during the 2001 Iron Butt Rally. "I had an overwhelming sense of doom about riding to Hyder, Alaska. I couldn't help it," she said. "Hyder was worth big points, but I couldn't shake the sense it would lead to very bad things. Michael didn't hesitate about changing our plans. We may have captured the bonuses without trouble, but trusting each other this way makes the trip more meaningful and enjoyable, and strengthens our sense of being a team."

There have been several times when I've had an eerie feeling—an uncomfortable premonition—about continuing with a planned route or course of action. In such instances, the feeling was so strong I was certain that if I'd ignored it, no matter how cautiously I rode, I'd regret it.

No one knows what might have happened if I hadn't changed plans—perhaps nothing. But I've heard of similar instances from enough riders whose opinions I respect that I recommend you heed such feelings. Whether such instances are metaphysical messages or simply your subconscious mind warning you that you're about to step across some invisible danger line, pay attention to them.

CHAPTER 3

Trip Planning and Organization

When I participated in the 1995 Iron Butt Rally, only one entrant in the field of 55 competitors, German rider Martin Hildebrandt, used a GPS receiver. The unit, which Martin had integrated with a laptop computer mounted between his handlebars, failed several times during the 11,000-mile event, a victim of heat and vibration.

By 1999 virtually all Iron Butt competitors had acquired smaller, more powerful, and more reliable GPS receivers than Martin's 1995 version and most were using route-mapping programs. GPS units have been available as options on some luxury automobiles and are beginning to appear as optional equipment on luxury-touring motorcycles.

The use of personal computers has become increasingly prevalent among long-distance riders, and many riders take laptop computers with them. Some riders only use their computers in the evenings after they have checked into a motel, while others keep them handy in their luggage and use them during the day as well, especially if they are participating in a competitive event and want to do some route planning. For such use, it's helpful if the computer has a "hibernate" feature that eliminates the need to boot up each time the computer is used.

Computer-Based Routing

Computer-based routing programs are an effective timesaving tool for planning trips—even for riders who enjoy plotting routes on paper maps with highlighters. I find it convenient to let the program calculate daily distances and total distances and to help determine places to stop at the end of the day, based on the distance per day I wish to travel. Since I usually pack my laptop computer when I'm on a trip, it's also easy to change plans while on the road. The program helps me quickly and accurately recalculate mileage and distance.

Automap was one of the first programs available for route planning. When you specify a starting and ending location anywhere in North America, the program will plot a suggested route—either the fastest route between two points or the shortest route, as you request. An advanced version of the program, Automap Pro, allows you to specify up to 100 intermediate stops, or waypoints, along the route, and the program will calculate the shortest possible route

Computer-based routing is a very useful tool for planning a ride. Many riders take a laptop computer on the road, especially if they are competing in an endurance rally, so they can modify their plans easily as they go.

This depicts the format of a typical itinerary listing and map produced by Microsoft Streets and Trips for a route from Durango, Colorado, to Gerlach, Nevada.

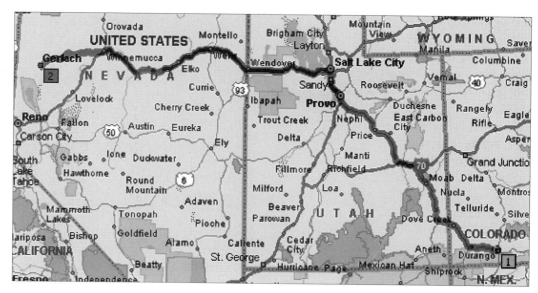

Summary: 843.4 miles (17 hours, 46 minutes)

Time	Mile	Instruction	For
06:00 AM	**0.0**	**Depart Durango on Local road(s) (North)**	**32 yds**
06:00 AM	0.1	Bear LEFT (West) onto 13th St [E 13th St]	76 yds
06:01 AM	0.1	Turn RIGHT (North) onto Main Ave	0.1 mi
06:02 AM	0.2	Turn LEFT (South-West) onto US-550 [Million Dollar Hwy]	0.9 mi
06:04 AM	1.1	Bear RIGHT (West) onto US-160 [Million Dollar Hwy]	45.0 mi
		Resurfacing near Cortez from 06/04/01 to 01/31/02	
07:04 AM	46.1	Bear RIGHT (North-West) onto Pinon Dr [N Pinon Dr]	0.3 mi
07:05 AM	46.4	Bear RIGHT (North) onto US-666 [Hwy 160-666]	60.0 mi
08:02 AM	*89.2*	*Entering Utah*	
08:26 AM	106.3	Turn RIGHT (North) onto US-191 [N Main St]	71.2 mi
		Reconstruction near Monticello from 08/03/01 to 06/28/02	
10:00 AM	177.5	Rest break (15 mins)	
10:15 AM	177.5	Stay on US-191 (North)	14.4 mi
10:35 AM	191.9	At I-70 Exit 180, turn LEFT (West) onto I-70 [US-6]	24.2 mi
10:48 AM	**206.0**	**Refuel before here (last refuel was 206.0 miles ago)**	
10:58 AM	216.1	Bear RIGHT (North-West) onto US-6 [US-191]	127.6 mi
		Resurfacing near Green River from 07/02/01 to 03/01/02	
01:49 PM	343.6	Bear RIGHT (North) onto Ramp	0.3 mi
01:49 PM	343.9	Merge onto I-15 (North)	28.2 mi
		Reconstruction between Springville and Provo from 05/08/00 to 12/31/01	
02:16 PM	372.1	Rest break (15 mins)	
02:31 PM	372.1	Stay on I-15 [US-89] (North)	19.3 mi
		Reconstruction between Sandy and Bountiful from 08/30/00 to 12/28/01	
02:50 PM	391.3	Turn off onto Ramp	0.2 mi
02:50 PM	391.5	Continue (North) on Local road(s)	10 yds
02:51 PM	391.5	Turn LEFT (West) onto SR-201 [W 2100 S]	17.4 mi
03:12 PM	408.8	At I-80 Exit 102, bear LEFT (South-West) onto I-80	215.0 mi
03:14 PM	**411.4**	**Refuel before here (last refuel was 205.4 miles ago)**	
04:46 PM	*510.5*	*Entering Nevada*	
		Construction in Wells from 10/01/01 to 02/22/02	
06:25 PM	**617.6**	**Refuel before here (last refuel was 206.2 miles ago)**	
06:31 PM	623.9	Rest break (15 mins)	
06:46 PM	623.9	Stay on I-80 (West)	118.8 mi
		Construction near Harney from 09/07/01 to 02/01/02	
08:36 PM	742.6	At I-80 Exit 178, bear LEFT (South) onto SR-289 [E 2nd St]	0.2 mi
08:36 PM	742.8	Bear RIGHT (South-West) onto SR-289 [E Winnemucca Blvd]	0.5 mi
08:37 PM	743.3	Continue (South-West) on SR-289 [W Winnemucca Blvd]	120 yds
08:38 PM	743.3	Turn RIGHT (North-West) onto US-95 [Melarkey St]	0.5 mi
08:39 PM	743.8	Turn LEFT (West) onto New Jungo Rd	76 yds
08:40 PM	743.9	Bear LEFT (South) onto Jungo Rd	73.8 mi
10:46 PM	817.7	Rest break (15 mins)	
11:01 PM	817.7	Stay on Jungo Rd (West)	22.9 mi
11:11 PM	**823.7**	**Refuel before here (last refuel was 206.0 miles ago)**	
11:41 PM	840.5	Bear RIGHT (North) onto SR-447	2.7 mi
11:45 PM	843.3	Turn RIGHT (North-West) onto Local road(s)	109 yds
11:46 PM	**843.4**	**Arrive Gerlach**	

that would stop at every one. The feature was originally designed for deliverymen or salesmen, but it's very suitable for plotting motorcycle trips—especially endurance events. The IBA began recommending the software in 1994.

The original versions of Automap and Automap Pro were effective tools for route planning, but the maps were crude. When Microsoft acquired rights to the software, they published an expanded version under the title Microsoft Streets and Trips that includes high-quality graphics for displaying maps. There are several other good mapping programs available and I've used them all, but Microsoft Streets and Trips is still the only program that can actually "optimize" a route that includes multiple waypoints.

To begin, you define the parameters you want the program to use for producing a suggested route, such as the speed you expect to travel on interstate highways as well as on limited access highways, arterial roads, and city streets. You also specify the time of day you plan to start and the time of day you'd like to stop, as well as the frequency and duration of any rest stops. For example, you can specify that you want to take a 20-minute break every three hours.

If you want to avoid interstate highways or toll roads, you can stipulate your preferences. Current construction information can be downloaded from the Internet before you begin plotting a route. To calculate estimated fuel costs for

The Garmin Street Pilot GPS receiver and Valentine V1 Radar detector are protected by the windshield and recessed into the panel John Laurenson built for his Yamaha FJ1200.

Even with computer-based routing and GPS receivers, paper maps can be useful for seeing the big picture, especially when you are in the early stages of planning a trip.

the trip, input your approximate city and highway mileage and the fuel capacity of your vehicle. You can provide the approximate cost per gallon that you expect to pay for fuel, or request that costs be calculated at a fixed cost per mile.

Once the program plots a suggested route, it will produce a map and a detailed, turn-by-turn itinerary that includes the time of day, number of miles to the next point in the itinerary, and driving directions from one intermediate point to another. It will also provide notations suggesting places along the route where you'll have to refuel. A summary indicates total driving distance for the route, travel time, anticipated fuel consumption, and trip cost.

Refining a trip is easy, as you can zoom into sections of the route to study them in detail. If you want the program to route you around a metropolitan area, simply include intermediate waypoints that will take you around the areas you want to avoid. Likewise, if you want to visit a particular town or attraction during the trip, include those locations as waypoints.

Depending on the amount of pre-planning you wish to do, you can request information about facilities nearby. If you know you'll be staying in Van Horn, Texas, for the evening, you can request a list of restaurants within some predetermined distance from the city, even filtering your selections to omit certain types of restaurants, such as Chinese or Mexican. You can also get information about nearby campgrounds, movie theaters, airports, and 30 or so other categories of attractions. Some mapping software even includes an extensive library of CD images of many national parks and other tourist attractions.

You can save your work at any time and you can save multiple versions of a trip plan if you're still undecided about all the details. When I plan a trip of several weeks or longer, it usually takes me several sessions of working with the program before I'm satisfied with the result. The final itinerary can then be printed so you can take it with you. You can also reproduce the map in several formats, including turn-by-turn maps or strip-maps.

Global Positioning System

The Global Positioning System (GPS) is a satellite-based navigation system made up of a network of 24 satellites placed into orbit by the U.S. Department of Defense. GPS was originally intended for military applications, but in the 1980s the government made the system available for civilian use. There are no subscription fees or setup charges to use GPS once you've purchased a GPS receiver.

The satellites circle the earth twice a day in a very precise orbit and transmit signal information to earth. GPS receivers intercept this information and use triangulation to calculate your exact location. The GPS receiver displays results on a small screen, providing you with a "rolling map" as you travel.

In addition to determining your latitude and longitude, the receiver can calculate speed, bearing, distance traveled during a trip, distance to some predetermined location, anticipated arrival time at a destination (based on current bearing and speed) and sunrise and sunset times.

The GPS system is sometimes referred to as an artificial constellation. Ancient mariners used stars to navigate and to find their way home; they

The view from the cockpit in the Colorado Rockies.

were out of luck when the sky was overcast and they couldn't see the stars. GPS, on the other hand, works in any weather conditions, anywhere in the world, 24 hours a day, as long as you have a relatively unobstructed view of the sky. Several models of GPS receivers are weatherproof and sturdy enough for use on a motorcycle, and a variety of mounting systems are available.

I was initially skeptical about the usefulness of GPS and I was not an early adopter. While living in Africa, however, I discovered that GPS units were necessary for traveling in the bush. Many maps of southern African countries list GPS coordinates to denote the intersection of roads and the location of gasoline stations and towns. I joined several 4x4 clubs and learned that members maintain catalogs of GPS coordinates for favorite campsites, animal watering holes, and other attractions.

I began using a GPS receiver for safaris and motorcycle trips through a half-dozen countries in Africa. It was so helpful that I continued using it when I returned to the United States, and I now use it for all of my trips, by motorcycle or automobile, whether I'm participating in a competitive endurance event or taking a leisurely cross-country vacation.

The Right GPS for You

GPS receivers are compact, powerful computers designed specifically for long-distance travel. Although experienced users reduce their dependence on paper maps, GPS receivers aren't intended to completely replace paper maps and atlases. Since the receiver provides a rolling electronic map, it isn't necessary to stop frequently to refold your tankbag map. But you'll still need to refer to paper maps now and then to see the big picture.

Opinions about the best GPS receiver for use on a motorcycle are divided primarily between advocates of small, portable models, such as the Garmin III Plus or Garmin V, or one of the larger Garmin Street Pilot models that were designed

Comparison of Features for Garmin GPS Receivers

	GPS III Plus	GPS V	Street Pilot ColorMap	Street Pilot III
Number of waypoints	500	500 (each with 15 characters for name, 50 characters for comments	500	500
Built-in memory	1.44 MB	19 MB	n/a	n/a
# of routes/waypoints per route	20/30	50/254 (auto or manual calculation)	20/30	50 stored (auto calculation)
Database or basemap	America's Highway or Atlantic Highway	America's Autoroute or Atlantic Autoroute	America's Highway or Atlantic Highway	America's Autoroute or Atlantic Autoroute
Additional map options (uploadable)	MapSource CD-ROM	City Select CD-ROM	MapSource MetroGuide CD-ROM	City Navigator CD-ROM
Battery life (hours)	36	25	2.5	2–20
Display size (inches)	2.2 x 1.5	2.2 x 1.5	1.8 x 3.3	1.8 x 3.3
Display type	4-level grey LCD	4-level grey LCD	16-color LCD	16-color LCD
Pixels (H x W)	160 x 100	256 x 160	128 x 240	160 x 305
TracBack mode	yes	yes	n/a	n/a
# of tracklog points	1900	3000	950	2000
Unit weight	9 oz.	9 oz.	1.3 lbs.	1.3 lbs.
Unit size (H x W x D)	5 x 2.32 x 1.62	5 x 2.32 x 1.62	2.2 x 3.2 x 6.8	2.2 x 3.2 x 6.8
Screen orientation	vertical and horizontal	vertical and horizontal	horizontal	horizontal
Backlit display	2 levels	multi-level	multi-level	2 levels
Voltage range	10–32	8–35	10–40	10–40
Waypoint icons	yes	yes	n/a	n/a
Garmin MSRP	$364	$536	$890	$1272

Seamans Jones

Prior to Seamans's entry in the 2001 Iron Butt Rally, this Alaskan rider had never been in the states between the Canadian border and Alabama, the starting point of the rally. He was also very unfamiliar with riding in the metropolitan areas in the Lower 48. Seamans was so intent on successfully navigating his way through the rally that he installed dual Street Pilot GPS systems. One served as his rolling electronic map, while the second displayed statistical information.

One of Seamans's goals was to complete the rally without referencing paper maps—an objective he accomplished thanks to his creative use of his laptop computer, the dual GPS units, and routing software. His Street Pilot III, which provides audio commands and prompts, was wired to his helmet speakers using a Kennedy Radar detector integrator that connected to his passenger headset plugin and operated through his stock intercom volume-control knob.

Seamans wired the Street Pilot III with a power/data cord combination plug that was routed to his laptop in the rear luggage compartment of the motorcycle. He could compute a route and upload it to the GPS receiver without touching the GPS receiver or removing the laptop from the motorcycle. He felt that this was a lot faster and it eliminated the possibility of dropping something. A small rain cover attached to his trunk allowed him to use the computer in the rain.

Although Seamans had a complete set of paper maps, he only used them once, at the beginning of the rally, when he was doing an initial review of bonus locations. ∎

primarily for in-vehicle use. All these are rugged and weatherproof, and have illuminated displays for use at night. There are a few fans of the Garmin Emap and GPSMAP 176, but these units have their shortcomings for long-distance motorcycling. For an in-depth comparison of the functions and features of various models of Garmin receivers, copies of user manuals, or on-line demonstrations, visit their web site.

The earlier models of both families (the Street Pilot ColorMap and GPS III Plus) lack some of the features of the units that followed them (the Street Pilot III and GPS V). These early versions are limited in the number of waypoints they can accommodate, which poses serious restrictions on plotting long rides, as the route has to be broken into segments. Waypoints also have to be specified individually using Garmin MapSource software (more on this later), or uploaded from a mapping program. In addition, distances between waypoints are calculated "as the crow flies," without regard to the actual distances by road. The V and the high-end Street Pilots, on the other hand, have automatic routing with turn-by-turn instructions, which calculates actual highway distances to the final destination, yielding a much more accurate estimate.

Street Pilots

The large, easy-to-read screens of the Street Pilot models make them very good for navigational use. In addition, they accommodate external data cards that can hold large amounts of additional information, such as detailed mapping and roadside resources, which can be downloaded from Garmin MapSource software. They are also very simple to operate, making them a favorite choice among riders who are new to using a GPS.

On the downside, Street Pilots are rather heavy units, and a rider must take care to mount them with enough support; the mounting bracket supplied for automobile use will only accommodate very shallow screws, and they typically fail when subjected to use on a motorcycle. Because Street Pilots are cumbersome, you probably would not want to use them for hiking and other such pursuits. Unlike the III Plus and V (discussed next) you cannot customize screen displays or automatically retrace your path using TrackBack.

Garmin III Plus and V

One of the first things you will notice upon comparing the III Plus and the V to the Street Pilots is how much smaller they are—small enough to be conveniently used for other off-the-bike pursuits, such as hiking, canoeing, and mountain biking; the batteries also last a lot longer.

Unlike the Street Pilots, the III Plus and V allow user-definable screens for displaying statistical information, so you can customize the display depending on the type of trip you're on. For example, if you're taking a leisurely trip across the country, you may wish to see your elevation, trip odometer, total trip time (stopped and/or moving) and the hours remaining until you reach your final destination, based on your current speed. If you're participating in an endurance rally, you may find it important to monitor a user timer and display the ETA at both your next waypoint and your final destination. Depending on the model, the same information may be available on the Street Pilots, but you'll have to page through several screens to see it all. With the flexibility to tailor screen displays comes a bit more complexity, however, and it takes some additional effort to master these features.

Both the Garmin III Plus and V also support TrackBack, an especially useful feature that allows you to retrace your path via a track log that is automatically stored in the receiver's memory, sort of like an electronic breadcrumb trail. None of the Street Pilots support this function.

In contrast to the Street Pilots, however, the amount of internal memory available on the III Plus and V models is relatively limited for long-distance motorcycling, though a less motivated rider might not notice such restrictions; they also do not allow the use of programmable data cards for expanding memory.

For my own use, I have favored the III Plus and V over the Street Pilots, since I value the portability, customizable screens, and the ability to TrackBack. In spite of these extra features, they haven't proven too difficult to use and I don't rely on the navigational benefits many of my long-distance friends like most about the

The screens on the Street Pilots are much larger than they are on the III Plus or V, which makes it easier to navigate from the unit.

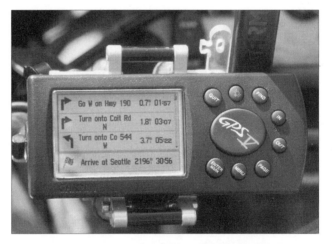

In addition to the information displayed by the GPS III Plus, the V also shows directional pointers, indicating where the next turns should be made.

Street Pilots. In practice, many competitive endurance riders equip their bikes with both a Street Pilot *and* either a III Plus or a V.

Garmin MapSource Software

Garmin MapSource software contains base maps for highways and roads throughout the United States, including such detailed information as the locations of service stations, restaurants, hotels, campsites, hospitals, banks, and more. Additional CD-ROMs are available with worldwide coverage. MapSource is used to define new routes, exchange information between your PC and GPS receiver, and catalog and maintain files of routes, waypoints, and track logs on your PC. You'll need an interface cable so you can exchange information between your computer and GPS receiver.

Some riders prefer to use a PC-based mapping program that can plot routes and upload them directly to a GPS without using MapSource. But routes that are uploaded directly from a mapping program use cryptic, meaningless names for the intermediate waypoints. As I'm traveling, I prefer that my receiver display a name (or a recognizable abbreviation thereof) rather than a senseless combination of letters and numerals. Second, I'm uncomfortable blindly riding a route that has been selected by a piece of software, preferring instead to exercise control over such things as whether to ride through the center of Seattle on I-5, or go around it on I-405. If I am going to take the time to carefully preview my route, I may as well plot it myself with MapSource and get the additional benefit of familiar waypoint names.

If you use MapSource software to create routes for the GPS you can also share your routes and lists of waypoints, including the locations of favorite restaurants and motels, special scenic areas, and other points of interest.

Putting It All Together

Mapping software and GPS receivers each offer sufficient benefits that both systems have become very popular in the long-distance community. A few riders use mapping software and PCs, but haven't invested in a GPS receiver. Others are advocates of GPS receivers, but don't bother much with PCs or mapping software, preferring instead to use models of GPS receivers that have automatic routing capabilities in which the GPS receiver does the route planning.

I believe there are significant advantages to using mapping software in conjunction with GPS receivers. My route planning typically consists of three steps:

- Plot the intended route, either with highlighters and paper maps, or with PC-based routing software. I use Microsoft Street and Trips, even though it doesn't support the automatic uploading of routes to a GPS unit.

- Manually enter the route into the MapSource software. The "drag and drop" feature lets you easily specify the beginning and end of the route, as well as major intermediate waypoints. If you plan to visit urban areas, you can upload detailed MapSource depictions of residential streets and local and county roads. A loop trip can be entered as outbound and return routes; if you plan to

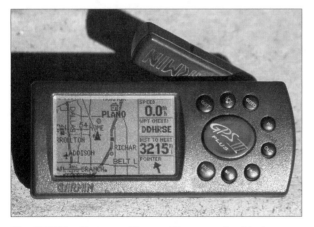

The GPS Map Page provides a rolling map of a rider's current position. In this example, the receiver shows that it's only 3,215 miles from the author's home to Dead Horse, Alaska.

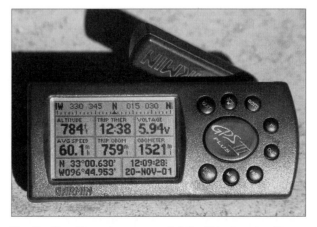

The Position Page shows current date, time, geographic position, heading, altitude, trip timer, voltage, average speed, trip odometer, and odometer. The six fields displayed in the boxes can be customized by the user.

return by the same route, you can "invert" your outbound route for the trip home.

- Upload MapSource routes to the GPS receiver along with any detailed area maps you've selected. Once you have disconnected the receiver from your PC and returned it to the mount on your bike, connect the unit to your bike's electrical system and you'll be ready to go.

It's actually not necessary to own MapSource software to plot routes into your GPS. You can enter exactly the same routes by using the rocker keypad. On occasions when I've traveled without my PC, I've plotted (or modified) routes in my motel room using only the receiver. Once you get the hang of using the receiver's rocker keypad it's not difficult, although it's much faster and a lot easier to do it with a computer keyboard.

Using a GPS

While you're moving, you can glance occasionally at the receiver's Map Page to monitor your progress as you approach waypoints. Of course, you should never fix your gaze on the GPS receiver for more than a second at a time without returning your eyes to the road. It should only take a few successive glances to find the information you need. I'm ever mindful of a remark that IBA President Mike Kneebone once made about GPS receivers: "The thing a GPS is most useful for is reporting the exact location of the accident you had because you were looking at the GPS receiver instead of the road." Mike has a good point.

Your speed will also be displayed on the receiver and it will be more accurate than what is indicated on your motorcycle speedometer. For that reason, I've come to rely on my GPS reading, and it also means I need only glance at one device. As you approach your next destination, the receiver will periodically change the scale of the map, zooming in to provide more detail as you get closer to a waypoint.

From time to time, you can refer to the GPS Position Page to see your average speed since starting the trip, how far you've come, your current bearing, or the time and date. There is no more accurate time than what the GPS receiver reads from the satellites, which is based on an atomic clock. If you want to see your approximate ETA for the day you, can access that information at the press of a button. In fact, switching between screen views, zooming in and out, and many other common functions can usually be accessed that simply.

One of my favorite features is the ability to quickly record the GPS coordinates of an interesting place I happen upon. Say you stop for lunch at an interesting restaurant in a small, quaint town. If you'd like to stop again when

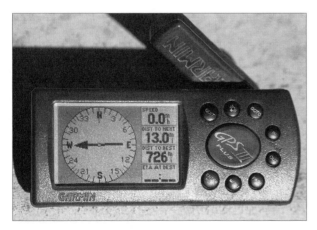

The Compass Page displays the current speed, the distance to the next waypoint, the distance to the end of the current route, and the estimated time of arrival at the final destination.

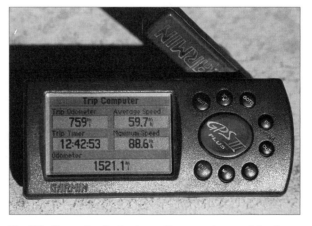

The Trip Computer Page shows the average speed (and highest speed) for a trip, and the trip odometer, odometer, and elapsed time.

John Harrison's rally-equipped BMW K1200LT includes dual GPS receivers and dual Roadbook holders. The Roadbook provides easy access to a large volume of printed route instructions.

you're in the area, you can define the restaurant as a new waypoint. It takes less than a minute to enter this information into the receiver; at the end of your trip, you can download it to your PC. As you continue your trip, the Map Page will display waypoints you've captured in the past.

But let's say you are coming up on a desolate stretch of highway through the desert. If you're curious about the availability of gasoline and wondering whether you can put off filling up or should take advantage of the next station, your receiver can likely display a list of the nearest exits along the interstate, with symbols to depict the type of services that are available (fuel,

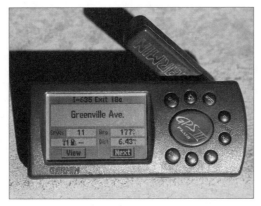

The Exit Information displayed by the Garmin III Plus is one of its most useful features. In this photo, the receiver shows that the user is less than seven miles from an exit that has gasoline and food available.

meals, lodging, garage, information, restrooms, etc.). Using the rocker keypad, you can scroll through the nearest 50 exits within 200 miles of your present location and the receiver will display the distances to the exits and their bearings.

As you approach an exit to get gas, you can activate the user timer to keep tabs on the elapsed time of your pit stop. I like to time my pit stop to see how it compares to my objective (an elapsed time of no more than seven minutes if I don't need a potty break—ten, if I do); I stop the timer just as I leave the entrance ramp and re-enter the flow of traffic.

As the day wears on, you can see what time the sun sets at the waypoints along your route. If you continue riding after dark, the screen of the receiver will be illuminated, so you can continue to use it. When crossing borders, you can change the receiver to operate in kilometers instead of miles, making it easier to keep in sync with the distance markers and speed limit signs. These and myriad other features will be well described in your owner's manual but don't be surprised if it takes a while before you can use everything a particular unit has to offer. The best way to become proficient with GPS is to begin using it for simple things and delve into more sophisticated functions as your experience level increases; most units have a simulator mode which will allow you to experiment with different functions.

Roadbooks

A Roadbook is a continuous printed route description in schematic form, printed on a narrow roll of paper which is loaded into a scrolling device that is mounted on the motorcycle. Roadbooks are used in many European rallies, including the famous Rallye-Paris-Dakar, and are used by some commercial motorcycle tour operators. Customers ride at their own speed, in small groups or alone, and use the daily Roadbook to find their way. Some motorcycle clubs in Europe use Roadbooks to run their riding events.

A Roadbook holder can be operated manually by turning some knobs on the device to scroll information along as the ride progresses. Motorized Roadbook holders permit the rider to scroll forward or backward at the press of a button. The holder is available with a backlight so the unit can be used at night. Roadbook holders and accessories are available from Touratech USA.

I know one rider who uses Delorme Street Atlas mapping software to print color maps, which he trims to fit the Roadbook holder and tapes them into a roll that provides up to 2,000 miles of

Daniel Cohen

Daniel Cohen is the undisputed champion of the National Parks Tour. In 2001, he accomplished his goal of riding a motorcycle to every national park in the 48 contiguous states, a feat requiring less than two years. His stamp collection now numbers more than 900 stamps. He maintains a web site that is a dream for National Park Stamp Collectors, whether mounted on a motorcycle or nestled inside an RV. The web site is at: www.danielcohen.org/stamps.htm.

Dan has also traveled extensively throughout North America. In 1999 he spent 100 days traveling through the 48 contiguous states. In 2000, he spent two months riding through Canada to Deadhorse, Alaska (Prudhoe Bay), the northernmost settlement in North America. He has completed numerous Iron Butt rides, including a northern 50CC ride from New York to San Francisco and a 100CCC from Jacksonville, Florida, to San Diego and back.

Dan is a freelance television producer whose work has appeared on The Travel Channel and Speedvision. Formerly, he helped create the cable television channel Classic Sports Network, now known as ESPN Classic. Prior to his career in network television production, he was assistant to Neil Leifer, the famous *Time Magazine* and *Sports Illustrated* photographer. Dan is currently developing and leading trips for Ayres Adventures, specializing in tours of the national parks and treks to the Arctic Circle.

Dan believes in spending a lot of time planning his long rides before he leaves home. "Before I ride anywhere, I plan my journey with a computer using mapping programs and a spreadsheet, he says. "I include route details, daily mileage, gas stops, gear lists, park visiting hours, service appointments, and whatever else may be pertinent to the trip. A little planning will take you far. A lot of planning will take you farther." ■

Obviously a long-distance machine, this BMW 1150GS has been outfitted with a 41-liter Touratech fuel tank and 45-liter tankbag (including integrated panniers), Touratech hard luggage cases, Bill Mayer seat, and PIAA driving lights and fog lights. When packing up, be sure to stay within the GVWR for your bike and try to balance your load from side to side. Keep your center of gravity low by stowing the heaviest items in your saddlebags or tank panniers. In this picture, the large duffle bag on the cargo rack holds two lightweight sleeping bags and camp mattresses.

route strips with detailed turn-by-turn instructions. Although this method is probably too cumbersome to be used during an endurance rally when time constraints are so critical, it could be useful for planning a long tour.

Packing Up

A checklist is the key to planning and organizing a successful motorcycle trip. The obvious benefit of using a checklist is that you won't leave anything behind. After a checklist has been developed, you can decide how to best organize your belongings into the available luggage space. There is considerable merit to developing an organized system that will allow you to find anything you might need quickly and easily.

The accompanying checklists can be customized to your own needs and riding style.

Carrying Capacity

One element of a motorcycle's design that's all-too-often overlooked when packing up is the Gross Vehicle Weight Restriction, which determines the maximum amount of weight your motorcycle has been designed to carry, including rider, passenger, and luggage. Staying within the manufacturer's recommended GVWR is an important element to safety, comfort, and reliability. Riders who select BMW or Honda's largest models of touring bikes generally won't have too much to worry about unless they are riding two-up while packing a lot of camping gear in addition to their luggage. Riders of most sport bikes will usually have difficulty finding a place to strap down so much luggage that they will exceed the bike's carrying capacity. Some sport-touring motorcycles, however, while supposedly designed for long-distance travel with two people, may not permit heavier riders to take much besides themselves before bumping up against the vehicle's GVWR.

An overloaded motorcycle will prevent the suspension system from operating properly, which means you will bottom out on bumps and you'll be more likely to scrape the underside of your bike during tight turns. Although this is uncomfortable and annoying, what's worse is that when the suspension system isn't working prop-erly the bike can lose traction, an especially dangerous situation if it occurs after hitting a bump or pothole while negotiating a tight curve on a mountain road.

Exceeding the recommended GVWR also subjects the motorcycle to more stress than the manufacturer intended. The vehicle's brakes, shock absorbers, transmission, and wheel bear-

Packing Lists

Riding Suit	
Inside breast pocket	Wallet, credit cards, currency, drivers license, proof of insurance, passport
Left breast pocket	Pens, small flashlight (pen light)
Right breast pocket	Miniature tape recorder
Left jacket pocket	Earplugs
Right jacket pocket	Lip balm
Right pants pocket	Loose change

Tankbag
3x5 cards for notes to be placed in the map window
Additional earplugs
Additional pens and highlighters
Atomic fireballs, spicy chewing gum, other small snacks
Cable and lock (for securing suit and helmet to bike)
Cell phone with built-in Palm organizer
First-aid kit
Flashlight
Hat
Log book/notebook
Maps that will be used soon
Spare helmet visor
Sunglasses
Tire-pressure gauge
Tread-depth gauge

Tail Storage Section of Motorcycle
CO_2 cartridges for tire inflation
Owner's manual, directory of motorcycle dealers
Roll of duct tape
Spare bulbs and fuses
Tool kit

Other
Shoes
Socks
Underwear
Trousers
Shirts
Bathing suit
Lightweight jacket
Spare batteries (flashlight, camera, GPS unit, tape recorder)
Spare ignition key, hidden on the motorcycle
GPS unit
Radar detector
Laptop computer and AC cord
Tire repair kit and inflation materials
Toiletry Bag
Zip-lock Bags
Dirty clothes bag
Camera and film
Electric vest and chaps
Extra gloves and glove liners
Additional maps and road atlas

Camping Equipment
Camp stove
Matches
Cooking equipment and utensils, including corkscrew for the wine
Folding camp chair
Sleeping bag
Air mattress
Pillow
Shower shoes
Tent

Helen TwoWheels

Helen TwoWheels is known throughout the long-distance riding community, especially among motorcycle campers, for development of her Super Packing System and products.

Helen (a.k.a. Linda Hedden) says that soon after her children were grown, she ran away from home on a motorcycle and never went back. She is now often seen at major gatherings of motorcyclists, where she demonstrates her packing system and promotes her products, which have been designed specifically for touring and for motorcycle camping. Her web site (http://www.helen2wheels.com) provides an excellent tutorial for packing a motorcycle.

Helen has some interesting ideas about riding alone, especially as a woman. "For me, riding alone is better. When riding alone I don't have to negotiate or compromise. When I'm tired, I rest. When I'm hungry, I eat. When I want to ride slow or ride fast—to either smell the roses or blast past them, I do so."

"I find that when you ride alone, particularly as a woman, people are more likely to approach and talk to you. When I ride with a guy, people talk to the guy and tend to treat me more like an accessory." ■

Helen TwoWheels (right) and Kristina Snyder are ready to hit the road with Helen's Super Packing System. (courtesy of Helen TwoWheels)

ings will wear out more quickly if the motorcycle is overloaded.

To find out the carrying capacity of your motorcycle, consult your owner's manual or specification sheet. If the specs don't specifically list carrying capacity, you can figure it out by subtracting the motorcycle's wet weight (weight with battery and fluids, but without a passenger, luggage, or accessories) from the GVWR. The result will be the maximum weight of the load your bike can handle safely, including rider, passenger, and luggage.

The following table illustrates the significant differences in GVWR for various models of motorcycles:

Motorcycle	Displacement (cc)	Carrying Capacity (lbs)
Kawasaki Concours	1118	500
BMW K1200LT	1171	488
Gold Wing GL 1800	1832	488
BMW R1150GS Adventure	1130	478
Yamaha FJR 1300	1298	460
Ducati Monster	618	457
BMW R1150RT	1130	435
Yamaha YZF-R1	998	432
Yamaha Road Star Warrior	1670	405
Kawasaki ZX-12R	1199	399
Suzuki GSX-R1000	998	396
Honda ST1300ABS	1261	381

Note the significant range in carrying capacity for these motorcycles. Although my wife and I aren't an unusually large couple, by the time we take our combined weight into account with our heavily padded riding suits and helmets, our luggage would be limited to about 40 pounds before we'd exceed the limits of the Honda ST1300—a popular sport-touring motorcycle. The Yamaha FJR1300, a similar motorcycle that appeals to the same market as the Honda ST1300, would permit us to safely pack an *additional* 80 pounds.

Luggage

How much you take with you and how you pack it depends on your motorcycle's available storage space and its GVWR. To help you stay within safe load limits, learn to leave unnecessary items behind and consider downsizing the items that you do bring. For example, when we're home, my wife and I use different brands of shampoo and toothpaste. When we travel, we share a small container of shampoo (her brand, of course) and one small tube of toothpaste. A hair dryer is a necessity, but it's a very small, lightweight model—not the large, heavy-duty one she uses at home. It all adds up.

Staying within the GVWR is important, but there are some other things you can do to help ensure that a loaded motorcycle handles well. If you pack your heaviest items in the bottom of your bags (preferably the side cases or saddlebags, which sit lower on the motorcycle) you'll help to keep the center of gravity low. Reserve the top cases and tankbag for lighter items. Consider what you put into the tankbag, as you're likely to be introduced to its contents very suddenly if you have an accident. This isn't the best place to store sharp implements or heavy tools.

As you pack heavy items in the bottom of your lowest pieces of luggage, try to pack about the same weight on each side of the motorcycle, so the bike doesn't become unbalanced. Also, be sure the contents aren't free to move around if you must brake hard and come to an abrupt stop. If heavy objects shift during an emergency stop or tight turn, it won't enhance your bike's handling characteristics.

It's also important to ensure that the bags you attach to your bike stay securely in place. I stopped using bungie cords for my large bags because they stretch when you encounter a serious bump and if you've secured any small objects between your luggage with them, the objects may fall out. I've switched to straps for the large pieces. I still use short bungies to secure very small, light bags to the lids of my aluminum hard cases.

Some riders still prefer bungie cords. If you want to use them and your motorcycle doesn't have convenient places on which to attach the ends of the bungies, get some Bungie Buddies, available from many motorcycle shops, and bolt them to your hard-sided panniers. The Buddies consist of a bolt with an eyelet on one end to which you can hook the end of a bungie cord.

Bungie Buddies provide you with eyelets on which to hook elastic cords when lashing gear to your motorcycle.

These straps provide a nice, clean method for attaching luggage to the back of the motorcycle. The bungies are used for small, light objects.

The Helen TwoWheels Super Packing System proposes a more elegant and workable solution than bungie cords. She sells straps that have been designed specifically for packing a motorcycle. In addition to straps that are long enough to accommodate several duffel bags, she provides short, looped straps with D-rings that can be secured to the motorcycle's frame to provide a way to attach bags to the bike. This approach is especially effective when you're packing camping gear, such as a tent, sleeping bag, mattress, and cooking equipment. Helen's web site has an excellent tutorial on packing a motorcycle using her system.

Many tankbags, such as this BMW Multivaro model, have an expandable gusset.

Finally, before you start off on your odyssey, adjust the preload and settings on the motorcycle's shock absorber(s) for the amount of weight you'll be carrying. All motorcycles provide a method for making this adjustment, and it can significantly enhance the comfort and handling characteristics of a heavily loaded motorcycle.

Tankbags. A functional tankbag is a necessity for long-distance riding. Virtually all tankbags have a clear plastic window on the top to display maps, directions, and other notes. A tankbag will also give you easy access to important things you'll need on the move or during pit stops. My tankbag typically holds items such as lip balm, sunscreen, eyewash, a banana or two, spare earplugs, a pen and small notepad, a flashlight, tire gauge, first-aid kit, cell phone, and a lock with a long cable for securing my helmet and riding suit to the motorcycle if I must leave the bike unattended. When I unzip the expansion gusset, I can even cram an entire change of clothing into the bag.

I've attached a strip of Velcro to the right side of my tankbag, and to my audio harness where it attaches to the helmet, so when I disconnect the harness I've got a place to affix the wire so it's out of the way while I'm refueling. If I forget to attach the harness to the helmet before I take off,

Yvon Gauthier loads his Hepco & Becker hard luggage cases prior to his departure for the 2001 Iron Butt Rally. Yvon had the aluminum cases painted to match the color of his motorcycle. Fellow Canadian rider John Ferber looks on.

at least it won't flop around and become damaged.

Integrated luggage compartments.

Large touring motorcycles, such as the Honda Gold Wing and BMW K1200LT, have roomy, non-removable storage compartments integrated into the body of the motorcycle. Riders need only decide which items to pack into the panniers or into the top case, and how to transport their belongings into their hotel in the evening. Although I've seen riders use large garbage bags for the latter purpose, a more elegant method is to use bag liners that are custom made to fit into the luggage compartments. Most motorcycle manufacturers offer these accessories. Less expensive versions are often available as aftermarket items. Bob's BMW in Jessup, Maryland, offers removable bag liners for virtually all types of BMWs. Integrated cases are usually waterproof and lockable, both nice features.

Detachable hard luggage.

Removable hard-sided luggage cases are available for many motorcycles. Some cases, such as the large aluminum boxes manufactured by Jesse, Touratech, and Happy Trails can be removed from the motorcycle, but they are awkward to carry. These cases are usually left on the motorcycle and bag liners are used to transfer clothing to your room each night. Some cases, such as those made by GIVI, are rather attractive suitcases when removed from the motorcycle, and most owners simply take the cases with them when they go to their room. Owners of this type of removable luggage don't need bag liners.

Soft luggage.

If you aren't prepared to spend the money for hard luggage cases for your motorcycle, a wide variety of relatively inexpensive, durable, waterproof soft-sided luggage is available. Owners of some models of sport bikes and cruisers have limited options when it comes to hard luggage, and soft luggage may be their only reasonable alternative. In the simplest designs, saddlebags are slung over the seat via straps. There is usually some method to attach the bags to the frame of the motorcycle or to the passenger footpegs for more stability. Since it's impractical to lock soft-sided luggage to the

Bag liners that are custom fitted to your panniers make it easy to keep all of your luggage together. The liners make it convenient to transfer luggage from your motorcycle to your hotel room.

The large tankbag with integrated panniers on this dual-sport motorcycle holds 45 liters. The panniers provide additional storage down low, helping keep the center of gravity low.

Hard-sided aluminum luggage cases, such as these models from Touratech, are popular among off-highway riders. They provide as much as twice the capacity of stock bags and are much sturdier. Obviously, they are designed to be functional, not pretty.

motorcycle, you simply take it all into your motel in the evening.

If you still need added capacity after filling up your tankbag and panniers (and any rider who plans to camp from the motorcycle certainly will) you can stack waterproof duffel bags on the back of the motorcycle. When riding two-up, you can expand your cargo capacity by strapping small duffel bags to the top of hard-sided panniers, but try to restrict this to lightweight objects.

Be Prepared

The importance of carrying a good first-aid kit and the equipment needed to fix a punctured tire was discussed in Chapter 2: Safety. And few riders need to be convinced of the value of a cell phone when things aren't going as planned. Some additional precautions can make your long trips more enjoyable.

Credit Cards

Some riders are surprised to learn, during the course of a long trip, that authorization for their credit card purchases will be suddenly denied. Thieves often test stolen cards by purchasing a few gallons of gas at a pay-at-the-pump station; if the card works, suggesting that its loss hasn't been reported, the thief will then use the card for

a larger purchase. When the computer programs used by credit card companies detect this or any other buying pattern that seems out of the ordinary, the company will attempt to contact you. If you aren't home to take the call, future purchases can be rejected.

Riders who make gasoline purchases in several different states in the same day create a suspicious scenario to a credit card company. To prevent having your purchases denied, contact your credit card company prior to leaving for an extended trip, explain that you'll be traveling through many states and will be using the credit card for frequent, relatively small purchases at gasoline stations, and request that they annotate your file so your pattern of use doesn't trigger their security system to reject your purchases. Of course, you should carry a backup card from a different credit card issuer, just in case.

When You Need Help

As you venture farther and farther from home, it becomes increasingly important to prepare for a mechanical breakdown, a puncture that you aren't able to repair, or other mishap that leaves you stranded. You have two choices: appeal to a nearby member of a volunteer program who has agreed to help stranded riders, or call a roadside assistance program to which you had the foresight to subscribe before your trip.

The American Motorcyclist Association (AMA), the BMW Motorcycle Owners of America (BMWMOA), and the Gold Wing Road Riders Association (GWRRA) sponsor programs whereby members who need help can quickly contact a member who has volunteered to assist a stranded rider.

If you've joined the AMA's Help 'N Hands program, you can call a toll-free number from anywhere in the United States or Canada—24 hours a day, 7 days a week—and an operator will give you the telephone numbers of the closest Help 'N Hands members. If you're a member of BMWMOA or GWRRA, you can refer to the *Anonymous Book* or the *Gold Book,* respectively, to find the phone numbers of the nearest volunteers. The books don't provide names or street addresses, but they indicate the type of help available and the distance the person would be willing to travel to provide assistance. For example, the *Anonymous Book* indicates whether the volunteer has the space or tools for you to work on your motorcycle, whether a trailer is available, and so on.

Although the BMWMOA services are intended for owners of BMW motorcycles, the AMA program is available to owners of all brands. The GWRRA permits riders who don't

Iron Butt competitor Morris Kruemcke's Gold Wing 1800 has been set up with two GPS receivers, a cell phone, wide-angle mirrors, and a sheet of plexiglass that Morris uses to record notes.

own a Gold Wing (or even a Honda) to join on an associate-member basis.

The AMA, BMWMOA, GWRRA, HOG (Harley Owners Group), and the HRCA (Honda Rider's Club of America) offer members roadside assistance programs. Toll-free phone numbers are provided for the United States and

A soft cooler chest augmented with some straps creates additional storage space around the auxiliary fuel tank.

When you are far from home and help, it's good to be prepared for just about anything you could encounter.

Canada—24 hours a day, 7 days a week—to thousands of towing services. These programs generally entail an annual fee in addition to the club's membership fee.

If you're already a member of The American Automobile Association (AAA), you can sign up for their Enhanced Roadside Assistance Benefits with AAA Plus and have your motorcycle covered along with your automobile. In addition to towing, AAA offers members emergency fuel delivery in case you permit yourself to run out.

The LDRider Internet group also has a help list specifically for long-distance enthusiasts.

Members also provide certification services for riders who wish to earn Iron Butt Association recognition for certified rides. The list is patterned after the BMW Anonymous program, except that periodic distribution of the list, via an Excel spreadsheet, is limited to members who have signed up to be available to help others. At the time of this printing, there were more than 400 subscribers to the list.

As you extend your travels farther and farther from home, you may appreciate the additional peace of mind that these services provide.

CHAPTER 4

Building Mileage

The single most important piece of advice I can give riders who wish to build their daily mileage is to start slowly and increase gradually, which will give you an opportunity to learn how you can best handle high-mileage days. Is your seat sufficiently comfortable or is a seat pad or a custom seat required? Does your windshield and fairing provide enough protection, or should it be adjusted or replaced? Are your earplugs comfortable? Is your riding suit weatherproof? At approximately what temperatures will you require electric clothing? How much sleep do you need after spending a long day in the saddle?

As total daily mileage becomes a priority, many riders make additional modifications to their motorcycles which allow them to stay in the saddle even longer; auxiliary fuel cells are popular additions. With the idea of spending more time on their bikes, long-distance riders typically have a supply of water (up to a gallon) that can be taken while moving, and they often carry food and snacks to eat on the move. Veterans also concentrate on honing their routines at pit stops. Although speed won't be as important as consistency, those who push their luck with speed limits often equip their motorcycles with radar detectors and CB radios.

Iron Butt Association Awards

For many riders, the enjoyment of being on the motorcycle mile after mile is its own reward. Others find that riding-associated goals give them benchmarks against which to measure themselves. Several motorcycling organizations offer achievement awards in recognition of meeting specific riding objectives. The world's

preeminent long-distance motorcycle touring group is the Iron Butt Association. The IBA sponsors many rides which motorcyclists may do at their own pace, whenever they wish.

The IBA awards certificates of accomplishment and membership to riders who provide proof of having completed certain "milestone" rides. To qualify, a rider must obtain signatures of witnesses at the beginning and end of the ride, along with gasoline receipts to indicate where fuel was purchased along the route. Anyone can attempt an Iron Butt ride by printing a copy of the necessary paperwork from the Iron Butt web

For riders like Tony Black, whose summer vacations take him to the Yukon and Alaska, the Signpost Forest at Watson Lake is a "must-see." The tradition of a visitor hanging a sign from his home town was started by a homesick GI in 1942. Today, there are nearly 50,000 signs from communities all over the world.

site, which also lists the rules associated with the ride.

The Long-Distance Riders' Help List provides an Internet-based directory of volunteers from the long-distance community who have agreed to be available to witness IBA award rides. The list contains the names of long-distance enthusiasts from around the world, so you're likely to be able to locate a volunteer close to you, no matter where you intend to begin and end your ride.

Upon successfully completing a ride, you will receive a certificate, suitable for framing, membership in the IBA, and a listing of your accomplishment on the Iron Butt web site, along with several thousand other riders who have earned Iron Butt certificates. Once a member of the IBA, you are entitled to purchase an Iron Butt license tag frame for your motorcycle. Some rallymasters require that a rider has previously earned an Iron Butt certificate to be eligible for participation in endurance rallies that they sponsor.

The popularity of long-distance riding has exploded in recent years. In 1995, only 38 riders obtained an IBA (Iron Butt Association)

Brazilian rider Alvaro Teixeira was the first South American rider to earn a Bun Burner Gold certificate.

SaddleSore certificate for riding 1,000 miles in 24 hours. Four riders received a Bun Burner Gold certificate for riding 1,500 miles in 24 hours and only one 50CC certificate was issued for riding coast-to-coast in less than 50 hours. Five years later, the IBA issued 1,500 SaddleSore certificates, 250 Bun Burner Gold certificates, and added the names of *fifty* riders to the list of 50CC finishers.

National Parks Tour Master Traveler

Iron Butt Association President Michael Kneebone was thrilled when he learned that more than 500 national park "passport stamps" are available at U.S. National Parks. Park visitors can purchase a passport booklet and get it stamped whenever they visit a park. Mike developed a special award for motorcyclists who visit national parks and collect the stamps. The Iron Butt Association National Parks Tour Master Traveler Award requires riders to have their passport booklets stamped at a minimum of 50 national parks, in at least 25 states, within a year. Riders may begin their tour anytime and may visit the national parks according to their own schedule, however. The U.S. Park Service maintains a web site with a detailed directory of national parks and national monuments.

In addition to the IBA National Parks Award, riders looking for interesting places to ride can

Certificate	Requirements
SaddleSore 1,000	1,000 miles or more in 24 hours or less
Bun Burner	1,500 miles or more in 36 hours or less
SaddleSore 2,000	Two SaddleSores, back-to-back
Bun Burner Gold	1,500 miles or more in 24 hours or less
Bun Burner Gold 3,000	Two Bun Burner Golds, back-to-back
50CC Quest	Coast-to-Coast (Atlantic to Pacific, or vice-versa) in 50 hours or less
CCC Gold	Two 50CC Quests back-to-back
SaddleSore 5,000	5,000 miles or more in five days or less
Trans-Canadian Gold	Vancouver, BC, to Halifax, NS, (or the reverse) in less than 75 hours.
10/10ths	10,000 miles or more in ten days or less
Alaska plus 48	Visit the 49 North American states in ten days or less
Master Traveler	Visit at least 50 U.S. National Parks in 25 states within a year
Forty-Eight State Tour	Visit the 48 contiguous states in ten days or less
Ultimate Coast-to-Coast	Key West, FL, to Prudhoe Bay, AK, (or the reverse) in less than ten days
100K Club	Ride 100,000 miles in one year

The Iron Butt Association awards certificates for these rides, all of which include membership in the Iron Butt Association.

Some Iron Butters have become committed to building a collection of certificates by completing numerous rides that the association recognizes.

refer to the Scenic Byways web site maintained by the U.S. Department of Transportation. The site includes a directory of some of the most beautiful and interesting highways in America's Scenic Byways Program.

Four Corners Tour

The Southern California Motorcycle Association sponsors the Four Corners Tour, for which a rider must show evidence of having visited San Ysidro, California; Blaine, Washington; Madawaska, Maine; and Key West, Florida; in 22 days or less. You may visit the four checkpoints in any sequence and by any route, and you do not have to return to the first checkpoint to complete the event.

After visiting each checkpoint, a rider documents his visit by mailing required proof-of-visit information in a stamped, pre-addressed envelope provided by the SCMA. The evidence includes a gasoline receipt from the checkpoint, a photograph of the rider's motorcycle at a prominent location in the city, the odometer mileage of the motorcycle, and the telephone number from a specified public telephone in the vicinity of the checkpoint.

To recognize those who have completed the tour, the SCMA holds an annual banquet in southern California to honor the finishers.

Ardys Kellerman

Ardys Kellerman may be a great-grandmother, but you won't find this Iron Butt Rally veteran sitting in a rocking chair—unless you happen to catch her at a gathering of motorcyclists at the Big Texan Steak Ranch in Amarillo.

With several successful Iron Butt Rally finishes to her credit, Ardys has completed more Iron Butts than any other woman. Her accumulation of long-distance feats began in 1990 when she set the woman's division record for the six-month-long BMWMOA annual mileage contest with 50,089 miles.

In addition to her Iron Butt accomplishments, Ardys has earned the 50CC Award for riding coast-to-coast in less than 50 hours and the Bun Burner Award. She has also ridden many 1,000-mile days.

Ardys enjoys the many "ride-to-eat" opportunities afforded by the long-distance community and finds that they offer a perfect excuse for spending a lot of time on her motorcycle. She looks forward to retiring from her job as a computer technician so that she can dedicate more time to riding. ■

Voni Glaves

One of the most well-known riders in the long-distance community, Voni Glaves has owned and ridden BMW motorcycles since 1977. She was the first woman to receive the 600,000-Mile Award from the BMW Motorcycle Owners of America and has been featured on the cover of *Woman Rider* magazine. The *Women and Motorcycling* exhibit at the Motorcycle Hall of Fame Museum in Pickerington, Ohio, includes an exhibit about her.

In 1999, Voni was the first-place finisher in the BMWMOA annual mileage contest after she rode 73,660 miles during the six-month-long contest. Her total was the third-highest mileage in the history of the contest—for men or women—and 1999 marked the fifth time Voni won the event.

Voni has found that the physical preparations necessary to accomplish a major long-distance riding goal are comparatively easy, considering the mental preparation that is needed.

"Getting my mind in the right frame was crucial since going halfway would be heart breaking," Voni says. "Six months of single-minded pursuit of a goal could be extremely difficult to sustain, so I did a lot of early soul searching to come to the conclusion that this was a goal worthy of the time and money and myriad intangible costs. I knew I had to eliminate the emotional drain of arguing with myself about purpose. Once I committed to my plan, I never looked back or second-guessed my priorities."

When she isn't riding, Voni teaches at a high school near

her home in Lawrence, Kansas. Her students seem to enjoy seeing their teacher arrive each morning in her bright red leathers, which have become one of her trademarks. During the summer, Voni leads North American and Canadian tours for Ayres Adventures and is responsible for developing their program of trips designed specifically for women. ■

Carolyn "Skert" Youorski is best known in the motorcycling community for the demonstrations she gives on lifting a dropped motorcycle. Carolyn shows much bigger riders how to lift a fully loaded Gold Wing upright by themselves.

Mileage Contests

Many motorcycle manufacturers recognize high-mileage customers with awards and pins for achieving certain milestones. One of the best-known award programs is sponsored by the BMWMOA (BMW Motorcycle Owners Association), which takes it a step further with an annual mileage contest. The contest begins on April 15, ends on October 15, and is open only to owners of BMW motorcycles who formally enter prior to the contest start date. The form, which must be witnessed by several BMWMOA members, must specify the current mileage for each motorcycle the rider intends to use in the contest.

At the end of the six-month contest, winners (in both a men and women's category) are announced, based on the number of miles they have tallied during the six-month period. There are no predetermined routes or waypoints a rider must visit—it's just a matter of riding a lot of miles.

In addition, BMW awards pins and certificates to riders of BMW motorcycles who have reached high-mileage levels, beginning with 100,000 miles and continuing up to more than 1,000,000 miles. Also note that the Gold Wing Road Riders Association recognizes "Safe Miles" with pins and patches. After riding 100,000 crash-free miles, riders receive a rocker to place under their Safe Miles main patch. If a rider is involved in an accident, however, he must start counting again from zero.

Ride-To-Eat

The long-distance riding community is renowned for luncheons and dinners that attract riders from all over the country. In many cases, motorcyclists travel from one coast to the other and back, simply to join other enthusiasts for a few hours over a meal. These events can be great opportunities for riders interested in becoming more involved in long-distance riding to meet others with similar interests.

The IBA web site includes a reference to the LDRider Calendar of Events, which includes information about these ride-ins, some of which have web sites of their own. Several of these events have been taking place for so long that they have become institutions that attract up to 100 or more riders. The most popular are:

The IBA's National Parks Master Traveler award recognizes riders who collect 50 national park passport stamps in at least 25 states within a single year.

- Feast in the East—Usually October, in Virginia or Alabama.
- Spring Fling—June at Café Veloce in Seattle, Washington
- Hyder Seek—First weekend of June at the Sealaska Inn in Hyder, Alaska
- Chiliburger Run—Early October at the Riverside Restaurant in Horseshoe Bend, Idaho

On the last weekend in December, riders from all over the country come to the Stagecoach Café in Stockton, Alabama, for the annual "last ride-in lunch of the year."

- Deming BBQ—Early November, Deming, New Mexico
- Stagecoach Inn Luncheon—End of December, Stagecoach Inn, Stockton, Alabama (the last ride-in of the year)

The Truth About Speed

When it comes to racking up mileage, consistency is more important than speed. Speeding excessively requires more attention and is more stressful than riding at moderate speeds, so you'll tire more quickly. Higher speed also equates to higher fuel consumption, which means more frequent stops. Finally, the time wasted while receiving speeding tickets will significantly eat into your average speed.

In the endurance-riding community, the "entry level" ride for IBA membership is a SaddleSore 1000—a ride of 1,000 miles or more completed in 24 hours or less. While the SaddleSore seems like a monumental achievement to the novice long-distance rider, veteran riders can finish this ride in 18 hours or less while traveling within the speed limit.

The following table depicts how such a ride might be performed, riding at a consistent average of 65 miles per hour, with pit stops that reduce the average speed to less than 60 mph:

	Start	Stop	Mins.	Cum. Avg. Speed	Miles
Ride	05:00	08:00	180	65	195
Pit Stop	08:00	08:07	7		
Ride	08:07	11:00	173	63.7	382
Lunch	11:00	11:30	30		
Ride	11:30	14:30	180	60.8	577
Pit Stop	14:30	14:40	10		
Ride	14:40	17:40	180	60.9	772
Pit Stop	17:40	17:50	10		
Ride	17:50	20:50	180	61.1	967
Dinner	20:50	21:20	30		
Ride	21:20	22:00	40	59.5	1,011

This example assumes average pit stops of between seven and ten minutes each and leisurely stops of 30 minutes for lunch and dinner.

The Bun Burner Gold is a more challenging ride. It demands that a rider travel 1,500 miles in 24 hours or less. As the following table shows, this ride may also be completed without exceeding a 70-mile-per-hour speed, provided the rider makes relatively short pit stops and takes less time for meals.

	Start	Stop	Mins.	Cum. Avg. Speed	Miles
Ride	05:00	08:00	180	70	210
Pit Stop	08:00	08:07	7		
Ride	08:07	11:00	173	68.7	412
Lunch	11:00	11:15	15		
Ride	11:15	14:30	195	67.3	639
Pit Stop	14:30	14:40	10		
Ride	14:40	17:40	180	67.1	849
Pit Stop	17:40	17:50	10		
Ride	17:50	20:50	180	66.9	1,059
Dinner	20:50	21:05	15		
Ride	21:05	00:05	180	66.5	1,269
Pit Stop	00:05	00:15	10		
Ride	00:15	03:00	165	66.4	1,462
Pit Stop	03:00	03:07	7		
Ride	03:07	04:00	53	66.3	1,524

Endurance-minded riders from around the world visit the United States to participate in Iron Butt sponsored rides. With interstate highways and the wide open spaces of the American West, the United States offers endurance-riding opportunities that are unequaled in the rest of the world. British endurance rider Mik Reed flew to the United States and borrowed a motorcycle to do an IBA 50CC ride from Jacksonville, Florida, to San Diego, California. Mik (left) and the author are pictured at the Palo Duro Canyon in Texas.

This route through southwest Texas takes riders into Big Bend National Park.

For both of these rides, it's assumed that the motorcycle was not equipped with auxiliary fuel and was required to stop about every 200 miles; riders with auxiliary fuel can do the ride a bit more easily.

Avoiding Tickets

The best way to avoid "performance awards" is to stay within five miles per hour of posted speed limits and to avoid driving recklessly. Most law-enforcement officers won't stop a vehicle that is within five miles per hour of the posted speed limit (sometimes as many as ten miles per hour), unless the vehicle is being driven recklessly or aggressively.

Your driving behavior can also influence whether or not you attract the attention of law enforcement officers. Although I recommend that you stay in the left lane and travel slightly faster than the flow of traffic when the traffic is heavy, you should ride differently when you're pound-ing the superslab in light traffic; stay in the right lane except when you are passing. When there are few cars on the road, vehicles attract more attention from police when they travel express-ways in the left lane.

Calibrating Your Speedometer

If you wish to limit your speeds to "five over," you should understand that virtually all motor-cycle speedometers read more than actual speed. The most convenient way to determine the accuracy of a motorcycle's speedometer is to check it with a GPS receiver. So long as you're traveling in a fairly straight line at a fairly constant speed, the GPS-indicated speed will be very accurate. If you don't own a GPS receiver, you can calibrate your speedometer using either a measured course, sometimes found along interstate highways, or mile markers.

Most measured courses are five miles or less in length. Five miles is the minimum distance

Heidi Weldon

Along with Voni Glaves, Ardys Kellerman, Linda Babcock, and Linda Hedden (a.k.a. "Helen TwoWheels"), Heidi Weldon has helped women dominate the BMW Mileage Contest for the past several years. Of the more than 1,700 members who started the 2000 contest, Heidi was the overall winner, riding 55,579 miles between mid-April and mid-October.

Heidi racked up many of the miles from her participation in the Waltz Across Texas, the Four Corners Tour, Top of the Rockies, Rattlesnake 2000, Gerlachfest's group SaddleSore, and the I've Been Everywhere Tour.

A mechanical engineer, Heidi is a Senior Project Engineer with the Department of Defense—U.S. Army. She tests military equipment to ensure that it meets military specifications. Heidi is qualified to operate just about any of the military's wheeled and tracked vehicles, including the premier battle tank, the M1 Abrams. As Heidi sums it up, "They pay me to play with big toys."

Heidi has become proficient at crafting low-cost solutions for her endurance-riding needs. "The population of serious endurance riders in the motorcycling community is so low that we don't attract the attention of most equipment manufacturers," Heidi says. "We have to improvise. There are plenty of alternatives if you look for usable items in less traditional places. I made a shelf for my GPS receiver, CB radio, and radar detector from a plastic dish drain board. When I needed a waterproof box for my radar detector, I bought an inexpensive Rubbermaid box. Whenever I walk through a store, I take inventory of items I may find useful in the future." ■

that should be used to ensure accurate calibration; using mile markers for ten miles would be more accurate. To calibrate your speedometer, ride the entire measured course at an indicated 60 miles per hour, and record (in seconds) how long it takes you to cover the distance.

To get your actual speed over a five-mile course, divide 18,000 by the number of seconds you traveled. If you used a ten-mile course, divide 36,000 by the number of seconds required to travel the distance. For example, if you travel a five-mile course at an indicated speed of 60 miles per hour in five-and-a-half minutes (330 seconds), you would divide 18,000 by 330 to get an *actual* speed of 54.55 miles per hour. Thus, your speedometer would be off by more than five miles per hour.

Many speedometers are less accurate at higher speeds than at lower speeds. The following table can be used to calibrate your speedometer at various speeds, based on either a five- or a ten-mile measured course:

Bike's Indicated Speed	Dividend 5-mile course	Dividend 10-mile course
50	15,000	30,000
55	16,500	33,000
60	18,000	36,000
65	19,500	39,000
70	21,000	42,000
75	22,500	45,000

Cyclometers. Riders who want to determine their speed more accurately than their speedometers allow sometimes fit cyclometers to their motorcycles. These devices, which are designed for use on bicycles, calculate speeds based on the circumference of the vehicle's front tire. Assuming you measure your tire accurately, a cyclometer will provide a very accurate reading of your speed. Some cyclometers provide other useful information, such as time, distance traveled, average speed, maximum speed obtained, and multiple odometer logs. The most popular cyclometer among motorcyclists is the Sigma Sport brand, available at bicycle shops.

Radar

In the early days of police radar, it was necessary for the police to leave their radar guns turned on, since they required time to warm up. When on, the units emitted a signal that could be reported by a motorist's radar detector. Today, however, modern radar units have an "instant on" feature that prevents motorists from detecting their use prematurely. Officers surprise motorists by switching their units on at the last moment. By the time your radar detector's alarm sounds, the officer already knows your speed.

Most speeding tickets result from the use of radar, usually catching the speeder from the front, either by a stationary police vehicle parked on the side of the highway or in the median strip, or from a moving cruiser approaching from the opposite direction.

Radar, when directed toward a cluster of vehicles that are traveling together, cannot distinguish between the speed of the fastest vehicle and the slowest vehicle in the cluster. Instead, the radar unit reports the speed of the largest vehicle. Thus, if you're "hit" while close to (or while passing) a slow-moving 18-wheeler, the chances are that you won't be singled out for speeding, since the only certainty is the speed of the largest vehicle. If you're passing a large *speeding* vehicle when you're hit, be prepared to be stopped, however.

The perfect rabbit. You can sometimes take advantage of a vehicle that has passed you at speeds a bit faster than you would normally travel, by pacing the faster vehicle (the "rabbit") at a safe distance, usually a tenth of a mile or more. If the rabbit is equipped with a radar detector or spots a police cruiser, you can count on the rabbit's brake lights to warn you to slow down.

Sometimes the best rabbit you can find is a truck driver in a hurry. They are invariably equipped with good radar detectors as well as CB radios. Although you'll see them ticketed now and then, I think it's generally pretty safe to pace a fast-moving 18-wheeler, as long as you keep a safe distance.

Tom Austin

Tom Austin is an automotive engineer who provides technical assistance to the IBA. He has ridden motorcycles since his college days in the late 1960s. His interest in long-distance riding was spurred by the LDRider Internet list and by stories published on the Iron Butt web site. He now rides more than 30,000 miles per year. He rode 11,272 miles in 11 days during the 1999 Iron Butt Rally.

An aluminum auxiliary fuel tank is among the numerous custom-fabricated modifications Tom has designed for his K1200LT. To minimize the effect on the bike's handling, the tank is mounted low, behind the rear wheel, and is internally baffled. An auxiliary electric fuel pump is used to transfer one gallon of fuel per minute to the main tank through a tee in the return line from the fuel injectors. The 5.1-gallon auxiliary tank brings the bike's total fuel capacity to 11.4 gallons, allowing almost 500 miles between stops.

Tom Austin is a veteran of multi-day endurance events who has learned that occasional power naps of about 15 minutes duration are much more effective than the use of stimulants like caffeine. "Start drinking coffee or taking caffeine tablets and you not only get the jitters but your time between restroom stops is dramatically reduced," Tom says. "In contrast, a 15-minute nap will keep many riders alert for several more hours."

Radar Detectors

As mentioned earlier, little or nothing can be done to avoid being nailed by radar if you're removed from a cluster of vehicles and are hit by "instant on" radar. If you have a high-quality detector which detects the presence of radar from a distance, your unit may report intermittent signals from police who are working traffic well ahead of you, providing you with plenty of time to slow down. Don't assume the danger has passed because your unit stops chirping, however. If you hear a few short signals, slow down; you'll often ride for another mile or more before encountering the radar trap.

Your greatest risk is being caught riding "naked"—out in front of traffic and all alone. If it's

The cockpit of endurance rider Shane Smith's Honda ST1100 sports both the Garmin III Plus, mounted above the CB radio controls on the left hand grip, and the Street Pilot on the left side of the shelf at the base of the windshield. To the right of the Street Pilot is a Valentine V1 radar detector. Shown on the top of the tankbag is Shane's filing system.

been a while since an officer's radar gun was turned on to measure the speed of other vehicles, your radar detector won't have given you any warning, and when your unit fires, it will be too late.

Radar detectors are not guaranteed to prevent you from receiving a speeding ticket, but when used properly, they can help. The Valentine V1 is the overwhelming choice of radar detectors in the long-distance community. It reports the number of different signals ("bogeys") being received and the direction of the bogeys. To keep other vehicles from knowing you are using a radar detector, you can affix a remote display within easy view while hiding the detector inside your bike's fairing or tankbag. The V1 is not waterproof, so it must be stored when it's raining. Many riders have used Plexiglas to construct small, waterproof shelters for the units.

At most speeds you won't be able to hear a radar detector over the noise of the engine and wind, especially if you're wearing a good set of earplugs. If you have a sound system on your motorcycle which includes helmet speakers, you can integrate the radar detector into the sound system with an override feature that permits you to hear the alarm through your headset, no matter what else you may be listening to at the time. These override units are available from most manufacturers of motorcycle audio equipment.

Alternately, you could install a loud external speaker, such as those sold by SJL Products, which will help ensure that you'll hear the radar unit's alarm. An advantage of this system is that you don't have to remember to hook up your helmet to an audio system each time you're ready to take off.

Jammers. There are essentially two types of radar jammers: passive and active. Passive jammers, often advertised in magazines or sold by novelty stores, simply do not work.

Active radar jammers work, but they are illegal and can't be purchased in the United States. If you want an active jammer, you'll have to build it yourself. Homemade units typically incorporate a legal radar detector; when the radar detector picks up the police radar, it not only sounds an alarm, it also triggers high-powered microwave transmitters that emit strong signals to jam police radar. The illegal kits that I've seen suggest hiding the transmitters inside a fog lamp.

The March 1996 issue of *Car and Driver* included an extensive test of both passive and active radar jammers, as well as references to materials and plans for building the latter—although considering the expense and illegality of the units, I wouldn't consider using one. The test report, like every other one that I've read, attested to the worthlessness of passive jammers.

CB Radios. If I had to choose between a radar detector and a CB radio to help me avoid speeding tickets, I would chose the CB. Virtually all 18-wheelers are equipped with the radios and the drivers alert one other to the presence of speed traps. On several occasions the CB saved me from a ticket when police were using aircraft to monitor speeding. Truckers knew aircraft were in the air because vehicles were being ticketed in an area where no radar had been detected.

A CB radio can also help to keep you informed about road conditions ahead, including construction areas, accidents, and traffic delays. And, as an added bonus, you can be entertained by truckers' candid and colorful opinions on a range of contemporary issues, from how to deal with a cheating spouse to ridding the world of terrorism.

Some riders install scanners that permit them to monitor police radio frequencies. Based on conversations with those who have used them, however, I believe you would do just as well to rely on a CB radio and a quality radar detector.

When You Get Stopped

Riders have different opinions about the most effective approach for dealing with a stop. I've discussed my strategy with friends who are police officers and they confirm that it's a good approach.

First, when you know you're going to be stopped for speeding, pull to the shoulder and stop. If you're hit by radar from an oncoming cruiser and you see the cruiser execute a U-turn and turn on his lights, pull to the shoulder and wait for him. Forcing the officer to pursue you for a few miles before he catches up, while you

Keep the Gasoline in the Fuel Tank, Stupid

Before installing my first auxiliary fuel tank, I'd developed a habit of hanging my helmet by the strap on the right passenger peg, to keep it out of the way while I refueled the motorcycle.

Once while running low on fuel in Montana, I switched on the auxiliary fuel pump and proceeded to the nearest service station. The fuel pump switch had been wired to run whether the motorcycle's engine was on or off. As I pumped fuel into my auxiliary tank, the pump continued to fill the main tank to overflowing. After a few moments, I realized that the overflow tube from the main tank was located directly above my helmet and had been emptying into it!

I had the switch rewired at the next opportunity so that the pump would not run when the engine is off. But whenever I hang a helmet from the peg, I chuckle about the difficulty I had in fumigating the one I'd filled with gasoline! ∎

slow down and try to pretend to be surprised, won't help your case.

Don't make any movements that can be interpreted as threatening or suspicious. Remove your gloves, helmet, and earplugs and place them on the motorcycle, but don't reach for your wallet, even if it's handy. When the officer asks to see your license, first tell him where it is. I always carry my wallet in one of the breast pockets of my riding suit; I'll point to the suit and tell the officer that I'll have to reach inside for it. Most of them appreciate being told what I'm doing.

Don't insult the officer's intelligence by acting as though you have no idea why he stopped you or by denying that you were speeding. "When I saw your cruiser I looked at my speedometer and realized I was going a little fast," I usually say. "I'm not usually over the limit like that. Sorry." If the officer tells me how fast he clocked me, I wince a little, but I never suggest that he's got it wrong. After all, when I get caught, I usually *am* speeding.

I decided a long time ago to forgo pleading for mercy. The officer knows I would appreciate a break and if he's inclined to give me one based on my behavior, he's going to do it without my asking. Besides, I like being polite to the police, but I don't like to grovel. My approach must work because when I have been stopped, I've received verbal warnings about half of the time and I don't think I've ever been written up for the actual speed I was traveling.

Books have been written on the subject of how to beat a speeding ticket. Techniques include challenging the accuracy of the radar unit, questioning the officer's training in the use of radar, playing the odds of showing up for a court appearance in which the officer isn't present to

Mike Heren chose to expand the stock fuel tank on his BMW K100. This is the most convenient way to add fuel capacity to your motorcycle, as you have only one tank to fill and you don't need additional plumbing.

testify, and others. I've never been interested in going to such lengths to avoid a citation. Such measures should probably be used only if the ticket is about to cause you to lose your license. I'd point out that anyone whose license can't stand the weight of a ticket for an earned speeding offense has been riding too fast and should temper his speed.

Auxiliary Fuel

Some of the most prevalent modifications seen in the endurance-riding community involve increasing a motorcycle's fuel capacity. The easiest and most straightforward way of doing this is to replace your stock tank with a larger tank or have your stock tank enlarged to hold more fuel.

Since extra large tanks are not available for most motorcycles, you'll probably have to locate a metal fabrication shop that can expand your stock tank by cutting it apart and adding strips of metal. Many automobile body repair shops can do this work, especially if you find one that is motorcycle-friendly. An inquiry to the LDRider chat list can probably help you find someone in your geographic area willing to take on the job.

Before you begin cutting your stock tank, make sure the expansion won't interfere with the operation of your bike's controls or the visibility of the instruments. Also note that modifying your tank will probably reduce the resale value

Three-time Iron Butt Rally finisher Karol Patzer had the fuel tank of her BMW K75 expanded to provide a total capacity of eight gallons, enough for a range of between 300 and 350 miles.

of your motorcycle, unless you find another long-distance fan interested in buying it. You may wish to keep your original tank and have a salvage tank modified for additional capacity, so you can swap it back to the stock version when you sell the bike.

Although it is unlikely that you will be able to expand a stock tank enough to hold the maximum amount of fuel you're allowed, it is still a preferred method of adding fuel capacity. During pit stops, it won't be necessary to fill multiple tanks, and depending on the way your auxiliary tanks are configured, this can mean a saving of several minutes per stop. Also, an expanded tank won't reduce the amount of storage available for luggage and won't restrict you from carrying a passenger, as some auxiliary fuel cells do.

Saddlebag Tanks

Some riders have installed auxiliary fuel tanks designed to fit inside their hard luggage cases. The units are usually installed with a quick-dis-

French Canadian Iron Butt Rally competitor Yvon Gauthier modified the stock fuel tank of his BMW R1150GS to hold almost nine gallons of fuel. The tank was cut on each side and expansion material was welded in place to provide the additional capacity.

Mark Reis designed this custom auxiliary fuel cell for his BMW K75. The cell provides only a few additional gallons of fuel, but it doesn't detract from his ability to carry a passenger or luggage.

connect fitting so the tank can be removed when luggage space is more important than additional fuel capacity.

Champion Sidecars offers a tour tank that holds approximately five gallons of fuel. It's designed to be carried in a sidecar, but can be carried in the pannier of a touring motorcycle. The disadvantage of saddlebag tanks is that they make it necessary to open the luggage compartment to refuel, and the units occupy space that could otherwise be used for storing gear.

Do-It-Yourself Units

The approach favored by many endurance riders is to purchase the necessary components and install an auxiliary fuel system themselves, but unless you are confident that you have the mechanical expertise to perform the installation, ask a qualified motorcycle mechanic to do the work. If you have difficulty finding a local mechanic who is willing to do the work, contact the sources listed in the resource directory of this book for advice.

The following series of photos depicts the installation of an auxiliary fuel system on a BMW K1100LT, though the procedure would be similar for other motorcycles. You will need the following parts:

- An auxiliary fuel cell. Several sources for fuel cells, including Jaz Products and Fuel

Safe, are included in the resource listing of this book.

- A 12-volt in-line automotive fuel pump.
- An in-line fuel line filter. Although this isn't a required item, I prefer to install an additional filter between the auxiliary tank and the main fuel tank.
- Fuel line hose.
- A T-valve for splicing the auxiliary fuel cell feed to the main tank feed.
- A fuel line shutoff valve that permits you to shut off the flow of fuel between the auxiliary tank and the main tank.
- A means of securing the auxiliary fuel cell to the motorcycle. One popular method for doing this is to use ratcheted tie-down straps to secure the fuel cell to a luggage rack, or to a sturdy platform that has been constructed for the cell.
- An illuminated electrical switch for activating the pump on the auxiliary fuel cell. Usually, this function is relegated to one of the spare electrical switches provided on most motorcycles. If no such switch is available, a separate ON/OFF switch may be installed. It's important that the switch be illuminated when activated, so that the pump isn't accidentally left in the running position.
- Quick-disconnect valves to install near the fuel cell, as you will want to remove it occasionally.

The fuel pump, fuel filter, and hose can be purchased from an automotive supply store, such

Installing an auxiliary fuel cell, left to right:

1. A firm platform for the fuel cell was constructed of sheet metal and was attached to the rear luggage rack. With the weight of a full fuel cell on the luggage rack, the rack would have been unstable. To provide the needed stability, two small stanchions were inserted between the bottom of the platform and the body of the motorcycle.

2. Auxiliary tanks are filled with plastic baffling and sometimes pieces of the baffling break off. An in-line fuel filter will prevent wear-and-tear to the motorcycle's primary fuel filter.

3. Fuel pumps are available in a variety of different shapes and sizes from automobile parts stores. The narrow, cylindrical one used on this motorcycle was chosen because it could be accommodated beneath the motorcycle's rear bodywork.

4. The auxiliary fuel pump, nestled beneath the motorcycle's rear bodywork—viewed from below, with the see-through, in-line fuel filter to the left.

5. A brass T-valve connector mates the fuel line from the auxiliary tank to the main tank.

6. A "keeper" wire will ensure that the cap to the auxiliary tank isn't inadvertently left behind after a pit stop. Most riders with such tanks devise such an attachment, especially if they have ever left a cap behind.

as NAPA or Autosome. The valves are often used on fuel tanks for outboard motor boats and can be purchased from marine dealers.

After installing your auxiliary fuel cell, check to be certain that the platform upon which the fuel cell is mounted is firmly attached to the frame and that the fuel cell is grounded to the motorcycle. Ensure that the wire that provides power to the fuel pump is only "hot" when the ignition key is switched on. If you neglect to turn off the auxiliary pump when you park the motorcycle, you'll find that fuel from the auxiliary tank will be forced into the main tank and out the overflow tube. Not only is dumping raw gasoline onto the road or parking lot dangerous, the cylinders of the motorcycle can become so badly flooded that the engine is damaged.

IBA Rules and Restrictions

Most endurance rallies observe auxiliary fuel requirements and restrictions specified by the IBA. If you want to enter any endurance rallies, you should consult the rules on the Iron Butt web site before investing time and money in equipping your motorcycle with an auxiliary fuel cell.

Rules as of this writing are:

- The total fuel capacity of the motorcycle may not exceed 11-1/2 U.S. gallons, or 15 gallons for vehicles in the sidecar class.

- Additional fuel must be carried in a stock tank or an auxiliary fuel cell meeting NASCAR, IRA, or NHRA specifications.

- Stock tanks that have been expanded to accommodate additional fuel are permitted,

as long as the expanded tank is of similar material, gauge, and construction as the stock tank.

- Approval of other containers, including homemade containers, is at the discretion of the rallymaster.
- Auxiliary tank(s) must be mounted securely to the motorcycle. The rules allow proper fuel cells to be mounted on the rear seat, as long as the fuel cell is mounted securely.
- If an electric fuel pump is used, it must be properly wired and fused.
- The auxiliary tank(s) must be properly vented for pressure buildup and overflow.

Know When to Stop

The most invidious problem facing long-distance riders, especially those who ride late at night, is the danger of getting sleepy. A study of Commercial Motor Vehicle Driver Fatigue and Alertness performed for the U.S. Federal Highway Administration, confirmed what many endurance riders have learned—that drowsiness is much more prevalent in the wee hours of the morning than at any other time of day. The study stated: *"The strongest and most consistent factor influencing driver fatigue and alertness in this study was time of day because of the effects of 24-hour biological rhythms, known as circadian rhythms."*

The study found that peak drowsiness occurred during the eight hours from late evening until dawn. The study also found that time of day was a much better predictor of decreased driving performance than the number of hours spent driving or the cumulative number of days of a trip. Test scores affected by circadian rhythms and self-ratings of sleepiness were both worse at night. When compared to daytime results, tests performed on drivers revealed an eightfold increase in instances of drowsiness.

Ray Blair has equipped his ST1100 with *two* auxiliary fuel tanks, for a total capacity of almost sixteen gallons. Sampson Sporttouring Equipment installed the lower tank (behind the rear wheel). The other is an RCI tank from Summit Racing.

The fuel cell mounted over the seat of Pete Sutherland's K1100LT was built by BLM accessories. Unlike many K1100LT installations, Pete is able to continue using the motorcycle's rear top box for luggage.

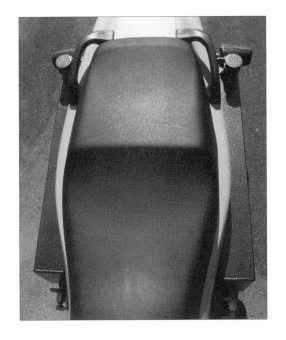

These auxiliary tanks made by Ron Smith add about two gallons to the fuel capacity of Cori Phelp's 1995 Yamaha Seca II 600, for a total of approximately 5.5 gallons. Since they are tucked away nicely, they don't detract from the motorcycle.

Warning Signs

You must learn to recognize the warning signs and stop to rest as soon as they appear. Warning signs include difficulty maintaining a constant desired speed, nodding the head, constant yawning, a temptation to close an eye for a second or two, deterioration of safe riding habits, and indecision over minor issues.

In a study conducted by the Stanford University Sleep Research Center, it was suggested that people's inability to judge sleep onset may be attributable to a lack of sufficient physiological warning signs in some individuals and to a failure to acknowledge the importance of warning signs in others. The study also found that even when a driver is well aware of his sleepiness, he might be so motivated to continue that he will keep driving despite the risk.

The Stanford study also found that there are times, particularly during extended periods of struggling to stay awake, when sleep can occur suddenly and without clear warning signs. Don't expect to judge sleep onset accurately. Be aware that you may not have adequate information from signs of sleepiness to avoid a sleep-related accident. Don't count on last-second warning signs or on your ability to fight sleep. If you feel that sleep is even *somewhat* likely within the next few minutes, pull over until you are sure you can resume riding safely and alertly. For more on this important topic, see Chapter 5: Getting Competitive.

Long-Distance Riding Tips

The IBA web site maintains an Archive of Wisdom, which includes an extensive collection of long-distance riding tips—as do other popular mailing lists, such as LDRider. In compiling what follows, I drew upon these ideas, as well as my own personal experience.

Count on Consistency, Not Raw Speed

Learn to stay on the motorcycle without interruption, at moderate speeds. Riding at breakneck speed between unnecessarily lengthy pit stops is sloppy, unsafe, and generally unproductive. Instead, develop skills and techniques to permit you to remain in the saddle for longer periods.

Get Fit

The most successful endurance riders I have known agree that the sport is more mental than physical. Although it isn't necessary to be a top athlete to compete in endurance competitions, it's a lot easier to handle the stress of long endurance rallies if you're relatively fit.

Bryce Ulrich's auxiliary fuel tank, available from Sampson Sporttouring Equipment, is a favorite among Honda ST1100 owners. It's mounted behind the rear wheel, to maintain a low center of gravity. The tank doubles as a miniature billboard for Bryce's favorite motorcycling organizations, including the AMA and the Honda ST Owners Club. Bryce earned the license plate frame after completing the Iron Butt Rally. The tag reflects one of his few complaints about the Pacific Northwest: the prevalence of wet weather. The side of the tank lists the many Iron Butt Association certificates Bryce has earned.

Eat Healthy

Fast foods and a big road trip are a bad combination. With minor effort it's possible to avoid fatty, unhealthy foods. Stop at a grocery store to ensure that you have fresh fruit for breakfast, rather than a large-calorie, cholesterol-packed breakfast. For lunch, stop at a Subway for one of their many low-fat subs. Denny's and many other franchised restaurants serve healthy chicken breast dinners, pasta, and other delicious meals.

Get Sufficient Rest

Know when to stop. When you're too tired to safely continue, pull over and take a nap or check into a motel.

Throw Plenty of Light Around

Make auxiliary lighting one of your first investments. Add additional lighting to increase your conspicuity and to better illuminate your way. If you're planning to ride through the night, invest in a good set of driving lights, and consider installation of an HID lighting system.

Avoid Last-Minute Modifications

Avoid adding accessories or doing motorcycle maintenance immediately before a trip. If it can be avoided, don't use a long trip or an endurance rally as a test run for a new motorcycle accessory, helmet, or riding suit.

Pack Wisely

Keep your sun screen, lip balm, eye drops, flashlight, tire gauge, maps, and other essentials in a handy location, like the top of your tankbag. If

This fuel cell cover was made by **Custom Tank Bags by Linda T**. It incorporates several pockets and a water jug with a long drinking tube. The zippers on the pockets are protected by storm flaps, which ensure the contents remain dry.

these items are not on-hand when you need them, you'll avoid using them.

Use Electric Clothing

Unless you're planning to restrict your riding to Texas in July and August, pack your electric vest. It doesn't take up much room and can make all the difference in the world when the ride turns chilly, even in the summer.

Use a Checklist

Maintain a checklist of items you want to carry with you and review it before setting out. Also, buy what you need before you leave home. Having to stop to purchase items once you're on the road can be an aggravating distraction.

Eliminate Distractions and Irritants

Eliminate all distractions and potential irritants *before* the ride, no matter how minor they seem. The cost in stamina and energy used in fighting off the effects of irritants while tired can be enormous. Even minor aggravations are magnified

Nick Sanders holds the Guinness World Record for fastest man around the world on a motorcycle: 19,030 miles in a recorded time of 31 days, 20 hours.

Don Arthur

In the eclectic world of LD-riding, relative newcomer Don Arthur has quickly established himself as a worthy competitor, expert at juggling time, distance, and bonus points to place well in several rallies. In 2002, Don completed the Four Corners Ride (Madawaska, Maine, to Key West, Florida, to San Ysidro, California, to Blaine, Washington) in four days, ten hours, and forty-two minutes—the shortest time by far in which the ride had ever been completed.

To pay for college, Don opened a custom bike shop and did welding, engine rebuilds, and show painting before moving to Harley-Davidson as a mechanic. A riding mishap put him in the hospital for weeks and on crutches for four years. After a dozen operations, he continues to ride with an artificial knee.

Don is one of the most personable, unassuming riders in the community. You'd hardly guess what he does for a living unless you notice the star next to his military decal. A Desert Storm veteran who served with the Marines in ground combat, he's an admiral—a physician with a law degree—and is the Deputy Surgeon General of the Navy.

Don loves riding all night, and dawn is his favorite time. However, he adheres to some good riding practices that help him remain safe while riding through the night. "The long-distance rider adage about stopping to go further is absolutely right," Don maintains. "When I become too tired to ride safely, I stop. And to avoid masking one of the most sensitive signs of fatigue—an inability to maintain a steady speed—I don't use the motorcycle's cruise control when I start to become tired."

Don says that of all the enjoyment he's had from riding, nothing compares to the enjoyment he gets from riding with his 17-year old daughter Lindsey, who rides her own Honda Shadow. ∎

If you wish to build your daily mileage, start slowly and increase gradually, so you will have an opportunity to learn how you can best handle high-mileage days.

during a long-distance ride, robbing you of energy and hastening the onset of fatigue.

Carry a Tire Repair Kit

The majority of tubeless tire punctures can be repaired in just a few minutes. There is no excuse for not carrying a repair kit, but even more importantly, you should know how to use it. Practice at home on an old tire so you are not learning on the side of the road.

While tube-type tires are more of a hassle, once you learn how to patch a tube, it can be done a lot faster than trying to arrange a tow.

Carry a Cellular Phone

They may not work in Death Valley, but you may be surprised at the number of locations where they do work.

Carry at Least a Half-Gallon of Water

You don't have to be riding in the desert to benefit from this advice. Even on a cool night, push-

ing a broken motorcycle a short distance up a hill to get it to a safe parking place can generate an indescribable thirst.

Route Through "Hot Spots" at Night

If your trip provides enough flexibility, catch up on your sleep during the day and cross the Mojave Desert at 1:00 a.m., not 1:00 p.m. You'll save yourself a lot of time and aggravation if you plan your bonus stops to pass through Chicago at 4:00 a.m., rather than at 4:00 p.m. Similarly, if you expect sub-freezing temperatures at night, plan more of your riding for daylight hours.

Get Gas Before You Need It

The time you waste looking for gas when you're about to run out, or the time required to find it if you already *have* run out, will eat into your average speed "big time."

CHAPTER 5

Getting Competitive: Endurance Rallies

Endurance riding differs from long-distance touring in two respects. First, the length and intensity of the rides are extraordinary. A 1,000-mile ride in 24 hours or less is considered an entry-level accomplishment in the endurance-riding community. Serious enthusiasts regularly ride greater distances, often repetitively for days, a week, or even more. Second, endurance riding is usually competitive. Whether trying to collect the most bonus points for visiting obscure locations during an endurance "scavenger hunt," or trying to improve a "personal best" on a ride from San Diego to Jacksonville, there's a competitive aspect to endurance riding that isn't generally found in other types of motorcycling.

There is some controversy in the motorcycling community about the subject of competitive endurance riding. The harshest critics contend that the sport should not exist at all. They argue that the sport is unsafe, as it encourages riders to continue to ride after they have become too tired to safely continue doing so, and that competitive endurance rallies are nothing more than unlawful races on public highways. There is a suggestion that the events should be morally unacceptable on the basis that the public safety is at risk.

Even some of the sport's most ardent and thoughtful supporters believe that competitive endurance events should not be publicized, but should remain the domain of a small number of riders who participate in them. I'm sure they dread the prospect of a book that generates additional interest in the sport.

If you are just getting into endurance riding, it's important to understand that the sport need not be any more risky than you wish to make it. When you go for a ride with a group of friends, someone in the group may ride too fast or too aggressively for you. Don't permit your ego to push you beyond comfortable limits. As with motorcycling in general, you alone are responsible and accountable for your behavior. Set limits that you're comfortable with, then stick with them.

Iron Butt rally competitor Willie Thommes left his companion Dexter at home during the Iron Butt Rally, but that's unusual. Normally, Dexter and Willie ride two-up in all kinds of weather.

Riding Responsibly

As is the case with most groups of riders I've known, there are a few reckless riders who turn any motorcycling event into a race. I don't believe the endurance-riding community has a higher percentage of such riders than other groups. In fact, anecdotal evidence suggests that the opposite is true. The endurance community scorns reckless riding and excessive speed more than do many sport-bike or sport-touring groups.

The IBA promotes safe long-distance touring. Mike Kneebone, rallymaster of the Iron Butt Rally, and most rallymasters of other endurance events not only discourage reckless riding and excessive speed, they implement measures to control it. These include suspending a rider who has been involved in an "at fault" accident from participating in events for some period. The staff of the Waltz Across Texas Rally use radar guns to set speed traps at key locations along the route. Although riders are given a bit more leeway than they might receive from the state police, anyone found to be speeding excessively is penalized or disqualified.

Rallies such as the Alberta 2000 and the Waltz Across Texas use formulas to penalize riders for excessive speed. Based on distance and

The Screaming Meanie is used by many veteran long-distance riders to ensure they don't oversleep. Those two circular areas on the front of the device conceal two very loud speakers.

time, the formula rewards riders for efficiency (bonus points per mile). The formula penalizes competitors who speed excessively to capture additional bonuses.

The Butt Lite was the first rally to introduce the concept of a "sleep bonus" and the practice has been adopted by other rallies, including the Iron Butt. The bonus is designed to reward riders for resting regularly during long rallies by awarding them more points for proving they have stopped to rest than they could hope to capture by continuing to ride.

Sleep

Perhaps the most critical factor for remaining safe while riding long distances on multiple-day trips is getting sufficient rest. Because sleep requirements vary so dramatically between people, the same regimen won't work for everyone. Some riders seem blessed with an ability to function relatively well with little sleep while others seem to function poorly without six to eight hours or more of sleep per night. Despite differing needs, several lessons seem applicable to everyone.

Experienced endurance riders don't consider it admirable to continue riding without sufficient sleep to remain safe. But it isn't only about safety. It's difficult to exaggerate the magnitude, seriousness, or consequences of the mistakes you can make if you've permitted yourself to become exhausted. Experienced endurance riders,

Roadside rest areas are favorite "Iron Butt Motel" locations. At many rest areas, it's possible to find a place to sleep that isn't too far from where you park the motorcycle.

however, have developed some effective techniques for getting the rest they need while avoiding the overhead usually associated with checking into motel rooms.

Power Naps

Competitive endurance riders quickly learn the incredible regenerative power of a short nap, often referred to as a "power nap." When the deadlines of a rally or the goals of a ride don't permit checking into a motel, a short nap at a roadside rest area often provides sufficient rest to finish a ride.

The United States Navy has done a lot of research on sleep and sleep deprivation among pilots. In their study titled *Performance Maintenance During Continuous Flight Operations,* the Navy confirms the regenerative powers of "combat naps." The study states that, "combat naps of ten minutes or more will help maintain alertness and job performance." The Navy feels so strongly about the importance of these short rest periods that the study states, "It is strongly recommended that commands encourage, and at times mandate, combat naps."

The study pointed out that there is some risk from "sleep inertia" lasting about five minutes after awakening, characterized by confusion, sluggishness, and a lack of coordination. But the research also showed that "non-habitual nappers" experience sleep inertia more frequently and that taking more naps (practicing) appears to reduce the problem. It's therefore critical, after you've taken a power nap, to give yourself some time to wake up and to overcome sleep inertia.

The Iron Butt Motel

Like many Iron Butt veterans, George Barnes restricts the use of motel rooms to times when he plans to sleep at least four hours. He points out that when you consider the time required for filling out forms, finding the room, and unpacking your motorcycle, the check-in process can consume half an hour or more. If George plans to sleep less than four hours, he checks into the Iron Butt Motel.

The term "Iron Butt Motel" was originally used to describe a situation in which a rider slept

Dale Wilson

Dale "Warchild" Wilson, along with Jan Cutler and Don Moses, co-founded the Cognoscente Group, an exclusive "by invitation only" endurance-riding group headquartered in Nevada. The Cognoscente Group sponsors open-class motorcycle endurance events that are open only to experienced endurance riders. Most Cognoscente events originate at Bruno's Country Club on the Black Rock Desert in Gerlach, Nevada—the acknowledged mecca of the endurance-riding world. In 2001, the Cognoscente Group captured the World Record Bun Burner Gold Group Record when more than 40 riders traveled 1,609 miles simultaneously in 24 hours.

Dale is known throughout the endurance community as a subject-matter expert regarding the Honda ST1100 motorcycle. He admits to having been an ardent pupil of the late Iron Butt champion Ron Major, who suffered a fatal heart attack during the 1997 Iron Butt.

Dale has earned numerous IBA certificates. In 1997 he placed fifth in the Iron Butt Rally. Manager of a large Internet Development Division for Lockheed Martin, he is webmaster for the IBA and serves as Technical Inspector for the Iron Butt Rally. ■

on a parked motorcycle, either leaned back against his luggage or slumped forward resting on his tankbag. Today the term is commonly used to describe any situation where you are sleeping outdoors near your motorcycle, rather than in a motel.

Rest areas along interstate highways in most areas of the country are relatively safe, although some areas have had problems. After several foreign tourists were robbed and murdered at rest areas in Florida, state police began assigning full-time guards to rest stops after dark. Another rider, an avid bicyclist and long-distance motorcyclist, prefers to use cemeteries to grab a quick nap. He contends that he's never been bothered while napping in a cemetery—especially at night.

If you're tired, it *is* possible to sleep on a parked motorcycle—but you'll probably be

Top three finishers of the 2001 Iron Butt Rally, left to right: Peter Hoogeveen, Bob Hall, and Shane Smith. This was Bob's first Iron Butt Rally, but Pete and Shane were IBR veterans.

The Iron Butt Rally has become so popular among endurance riders that there are always more applicants than can participate. Most of these riders have looked forward to participating in the rally for several years.

more comfortable off your bike. I usually carry a tarpaulin for stretching out on the ground. You can also nap while lying on a bench or table; leave your helmet on and place a pair of gloves beneath it to prevent it from becoming scratched. In the summer when you're concerned about flies or mosquitoes, carry a small piece of mosquito netting to spread over your open face shield, so you're protected while letting some fresh air in.

Although I've always found that the padding of my riding suit provided enough cushioning for me to nap for up to four or five hours, some riders pack a rolled-up sleeping pad with them. A few riders carry hammocks that can quickly be suspended from trees or rest area shade structures.

The Screaming Meanie

The Screaming Meanie is an inexpensive timer that many riders use to ensure they don't sleep longer than they intend. The device wails so loud that it's virtually impossible for even a very sound sleeper to ignore it. The Screaming Meanie, and its upscale cousin, the Screaming Beacon, can be purchased at most large truck stops, as the timer was originally intended for use by long-haul truck drivers who pull into roadside rest areas to nap. It can also be ordered over the Internet from Cycle Gadgets.

Stimulants

If you've reached the stage where you believe you need drugs to continue, it's time to stop to rest.

Most serious riders avoid using stimulants of any kind—especially caffeine. I'm so serious about being free of drug dependency while on an endurance ride that I give up caffeine several weeks prior to an event. I might make an exception to this practice during the final hours of a rally, when I might drink a heavily caffeinated soft drink or coffee. Many riders will attest to the temporary boost that a Snickers bar and a Mountain Dew provide when you're sagging from a lot of hours in the saddle. But the boost will be short-lived and the eventual letdown may leave you worse off than you were before.

Warning Signs

The most important piece of advice offered by experienced riders regarding sleep is to stop riding once you begin to experience warning signals. Although the danger signs were enumerated earlier in Chapter 4: Building Mileage, they are important enough to repeat:

- Difficulty maintaining a constant desired speed
- Nodding your head
- Constant yawning
- Temptation to close an eye for a second or two
- Deterioration of safe riding habits
- Indecision over minor issues

Bonus Points

Although there are some differences in the way endurance rallies operate, most are patterned after the Iron Butt. In 2001, the event started and ended in Madison, Alabama. Before leaving Madison, riders were issued a list of potential bonus locations to visit on the way to their first checkpoint in Pomona, California, two days and ten hours away. From there they would proceed to checkpoints in Sunnyside, Washington, and Buxton, Maine, hoping to arrive within the two-hour window during which the checkpoints were open. Competitors can arrive early, but are penalized a point for each minute they are late. If they miss *two* checkpoints, they are declared a DNF (did not finish) participant.

Between checkpoints, riders can collect points for visiting bonus locations, with more difficult bonuses earning higher points. There are usually more bonus locations listed than a rider could possibly visit in the time allowed, so strategy in planning which bonuses to collect is critical to a high finish. At each checkpoint, riders present specific evidence of visiting the designated spots, typically a time/date stamped gasoline receipt or an instant photograph of the location, with a specially issued and numbered rally towel clearly visible in the picture. At the end of each two-hour checkpoint window, riders are given new instructions and bonus listings for the next leg.

Trapped in an Iron Butt Motel

During the 2001 Iron Butt Rally, Bill Thweatt stopped at a small hotel near Winnipeg, Canada. The lobby had two sets of doors with a small space between them. Apparently the clerk had hit the lock button but hadn't checked to see that the outside door was actually locked. Bill entered the first door, heard the lock click behind him, and couldn't get through the second locked door. He was trapped between the two sets of locked doors and couldn't awaken the clerk.

Bill spent the next two hours trapped between the doors. He would probably have been there longer if it hadn't been for the hotel's cat. The cat was on the inside of the building and didn't like Bill being there. The night clerk finally came out to see why the cat was so upset. Bill, who was also upset about the incident, decided to continue on his way once he was freed from the hotel. ■

The format of the 2001 Iron Butt Rally is typical of the way many endurance rallies are staged, but this particular event included a few unusual twists. Riders could forgo the Washington and Maine checkpoints and return directly to Alabama—via Prudhoe Bay, Alaska, located at the top of the North American continent—to potentially collect a gigantic bonus. In spite of the enticement, few riders that year took the bait, feeling it may have been a "sucker" bonus designed to send them off on a nearly impossible mission—although the winner of that event succeeded in making the long ride to the Arctic Ocean.

Many factors complicate bonus selection and route planning. Sometime verification can be obtained at any time of the day, as when you need a photo of a roadside historical marker. Other evidence, such as a photograph of the rider eating "space dots" at Cape Kennedy with a specific rocket in the background, can be obtained only while the attraction is open. The point value of some bonuses can also escalate tremendously if combined with a second bonus of a similar theme. For example, competitors in one Iron Butt Rally could earn points for visiting either the geographical center of the United States at Lebanon, Kansas, or for visiting the geographical center of North America at Rugby, North Dakota. Riders who collected *both* bonuses were awarded an accelerator that multiplied the point values significantly.

Decisions, decisions. Endurance riding could be described as the sport of making good decisions.

Setting Up Shop

For most endurance rallies, the location of bonuses is traditionally a closely guarded secret, with riders learning of bonuses immediately before the start of a leg. Some rallymasters, including Jack Tollett of the 24-hour Waltz Across Texas Rally, distribute the bonus listing after the riders' dinner on the eve of the rally. This provides riders with their first major decision: whether to stay awake for a few hours to plan a route that will optimize their bonus points, or to rest in anticipation of making a more efficient ride. Riders who opt to go to bed are sometimes unable to sleep anyway and might as well be using the time to study bonus opportunities. Jack complicates the decision by withholding a few bonuses until immediately before the start of the rally. Riders who invest the evening in plotting a route won't know until morning how much the additional bonuses will change their plans.

A dilemma often faced by endurance riders is how much time they should dedicate to route planning versus riding. For short rallies, competitors may not have the luxury of spending an hour or two playing with scenarios; time constraints may demand that they get on the road quickly. For longer rallies, such as the Iron Butt or the Butt Lite, it may be wise to invest an hour or even two hours in planning a leg that will be two or three days long.

It's critical to have a quiet place to study bonus listings and plan your route without interruptions or distractions from other riders or onlookers. When rallies start early enough in the morning, you may have enough time before checking out of your motel to do some planning there. For multi-day rallies with several checkpoints, consider reserving a motel room in each checkpoint city. Riders who use this strategy will, of course, have to decide whether to arrive early and sleep until a checkpoint opens, or use all available time on the current leg to gather

Peter Hoogeveen

Canadian endurance rider Peter Hoogeveen is widely recognized as one of the sport's top riders. He's also one of the most pleasant riders in the long-distance community.

Perhaps the thing that Peter is best known for is the number of times he's finished major rallies in second place. He finished second in the Iron Butt Rally in 1991 and 1997. He's also finished the Alberta 2000 in second place. He's justifiably proud of his consistent high standings though, and is very good-natured about the second-place ribbing that he sometimes gets.

After his heartbreaking second-place finish in the 1997 Iron Butt Rally, I sent Peter a quote from Cicero: "If a man aspires to the highest place, it is no dishonor to him to halt at the second, or even at the third." I was touched when I learned, four years later, that he had made a copy of the quote and carries it with him in his tankbag. ∎

points and rest after receiving the bonus locations for the next leg.

Many riders believe it's smarter to arrive at the checkpoint early and get well rested before tackling the next leg. In multi-day rallies, the value of bonuses usually increases with each succeeding leg, rewarding riders who don't burn themselves out early. It's generally wiser to maximize the amount of time you can collect bonuses on future legs, at the expense of sacrificing bonus-gathering time on earlier legs.

Others, myself included, plan to sleep after the bonus list is distributed, reviewing it briefly before hitting the rack. I believe there is some benefit to letting my subconscious work on the problem while I sleep and leaving the majority of my planning for when I awaken. In either case, it's probably good to make a point of getting some rest before tackling your bonus strategy for the next leg.

In most endurance rallies, checkpoints are open for one to two hours, and you will have to figure out how to best utilize the dead time between when the check-in window opens and when bonus listings are distributed. Some riders use the time to replace tires or to make repairs. Others find a quiet spot and take a nap. And some competitors visit with fellow riders and spectators or to catch up on phone calls home.

Planning Your Ride

There are several key differences between competitive endurance riders and riders who simply ride a lot of miles. Because selection of bonus opportunities is so important, endurance riders will avail themselves of the latest technological innovations to assist in route planning and navigation; most are adept with a laptop computer, route-planning programs, and GPS receivers.

The merits of using laptop computers with mapping programs and GPS units instead of relying on paper maps and highlighters is frequently debated in endurance-riding circles. Most riders seem to make use of at least some of the technology that's available.

For me, bonus selection and navigation consists of the following steps:

- Mark bonus locations on maps while highlighting key information (point values,

With his maps spread on the floor, Ronn Moffatt is marking his route in preparation for the Alberta 2000 Endurance Rally.

During a multi-day rally, bonus locations are typically handed out before the start of each leg.

  hours when the bonus is available) on bonus sheets
- Use mapping software to select bonuses and plot a route
- Mark the route on paper maps
- Record the route in GPS computer software (MapSource) and upload the route to the GPS receiver

During the 2001 Iron Butt Rally, the most distant bonus stop was Prudhoe Bay, located on the Arctic Ocean, nearly 5,000 miles from the starting point of the rally in Alabama. Only Phil Mann and a handful of contestants decided to make the grueling ride, which included almost 1,000 miles dirt, gravel, and mud. The photo shows Phil displaying his rally towel at the bonus location.

Mapping on the go. Modern laptop computers are small and powerful enough that riders can use them during rallies to help with selecting bonuses and planning routes. When it comes to software, Automap Pro and Microsoft Streets and Trips both have an "optimize" feature that can select the shortest or fastest route between two points, incorporating multiple intermediate waypoints. For endurance competitions, bonus stops are entered as waypoints.

Automap Pro was originally introduced in 1987 on floppy disks and is no longer on the market, but it does have an optimize feature that operates very quickly, making it ideal for playing "what if" games with potential bonuses and rerunning the program to refine your choices. Microsoft discontinued Automap Pro when it introduced updated versions, culminating in Streets & Trips. Unfortunately, they rendered the optimize feature virtually worthless for use in endurance rallies. It might take Streets & Trips an hour to run a route that Automap Pro could have optimized in seconds. For this reason, many veterans continue to use Automap Pro, having purchased it when it was still on the market or obtained it through a reseller of used software or an Internet auction.

Other mapping programs allow a user to specify waypoints between a starting and ending location, and they will presumably insert them at the place in the route that will result in the shortest (or fastest) overall route. These programs do not perform an actual optimization routine, however. I've tested these programs extensively against the Microsoft products and they seem to work best when there are fewer intermediate points. If you cannot acquire a copy of Automap Pro, consider using Street Atlas USA, a product distributed by DeLorme. Although the waypoint insert feature isn't as accurate as Automap Pro's optimization, it's usually close, and carefully "eyeballing" the route selected by Street Atlas often discloses opportunities for manual improvement.

Before leaving home for a rally, consider entering "skeleton routes" for each potential leg into your mapping programs. Save them, along with other event information you have beforehand, such as the times you expect to depart the checkpoints, the speeds you want to travel, and the number and duration of stops that you plan to make for both rest and fuel. Also record the number of hours between the time you will leave each checkpoint and when you'll be due at the next one. Then determine the farthest possible destinations you'd be willing to incorporate into your route for any given leg, identifying such points to the north, south, east, and west.

Selecting bonuses. Although all riders don't follow exactly the same steps in selecting bonuses, this method should give you a good place to start.

Begin by spreading copies of AAA regional maps on the floor and use a highlighter to identify the locations of bonuses. It isn't necessary to be exact—it's only necessary to mark the city or town nearest the bonus. Some riders use three or four different colored highlighters and have a specific color to identify bonuses with especially large point values. You can also mark bonuses with small adhesive-backed paper dots such as those sold in office supply stores. The dots are available in several different sizes and colors. Some riders prefer them because they can write information on the dots, including point values or hours the bonus is available. I've tried the dots a few times but found that I always seemed to have covered up part of an important feature of the map, like a route number or town name.

As you mark the bonus on the map, highlight characteristics of the bonus on the bonus listing: bonus name, points, and availability. Later, when you're on your way to a bonus, it will be easier to page through the bonus listing to find instructions for locating and collecting the bonus. Make mental notes as you review the bonuses as to which have the highest point values.

Most rallies include bonuses that are impossible to obtain within the time constraints of the rally. If a bonus falls into this category, don't bother to mark it on the map. If you've already established skeleton routes before leaving home, and have already identified the farthest destina-

Manny Sameiro

Like many Iron Butt Rally competitors, Manny Sameiro looked forward to participating in the rally for several years. He attempted to compete in 1995 but all slots had been filled, so he went on a waiting list and was able to secure a ride in 1997. During the 17 months after he was chosen to compete, Manny overhauled his motorcycle to prepare it for the big rally, installing an auxiliary fuel tank, driving lights, CB radio, and a large drinking container. He upgraded the motorcycle's suspension, then practiced riding long distances as much as he could. He dreamed of a top-place finish—perhaps even a win.

With 300 miles to go before finishing the first leg of the rally, Manny stopped for fuel in the small community of Van Buren, Maine. He parked at the first of three pumps, which was labeled "Premium." Instinctively, he rolled the bike back two pumps to fill his tank with "Regular," passing what he assumed was a pump for "Plus." When he walked into the station after filling his tanks, the clerk commented that she had never seen a motorcycle that used diesel.

Appalled at his error, Manny undertook the time-consuming process of draining his tanks be-

fore refilling them with gasoline, then took off for the Gorham checkpoint, now concerned about having sufficient time to make it.

He experienced a high-speed wobble on I-95 near Houlton, Maine, and totaled the motorcycle after wrestling it onto the median. Although he was badly bruised and suffered some road rash on his arms and legs, he fared better than his motorcycle. Not wanting to wind up a "DNF" (did not finish) on his first Iron Butt Rally, he purchased a second-hand 1983 Honda VT500 Shadow—the only used motorcycle he could find. He bought some duffel bags to carry his gear and headed for Gorham, where he suffered high penalties for missing the checkpoint and for switching motorcycles during the rally. He finished in last place, but avoided the dreaded DNF.

At the awards banquet, Manny was given a new award that the IBA labeled the "Manny Sameiro Award," in recognition of his perseverance during the rally.

In the 1999 Iron Butt, Manny went on to tie with riding partner Harold Brooks for third place—the first time in Iron Butt history that entrants riding together finished in the top ten. ■

Reading Comprehension 101

Team Strange Rallymaster and Iron Butt veteran Adam Wolkoff has often said that endurance rallies are "all about reading comprehension." World-renowned rallymaster Jan Cutler can attest to the validity of this advice, based on his route planning during the 1993 Iron Butt Rally.

Jan was leading the field at the Spokane, Washington, checkpoint. By the time he reached Gillette, Wyoming, he was so excited about the number of bonuses he had collected that he called rallymaster Mike Kneebone to report his progress. He closed the conversation by confirming that he'd see Mike at the Chicago checkpoint the next evening.

Mike pointed out that the checkpoint would be closed in the evening, as it was scheduled to be open from 9:00 a.m. to 11:00 a.m.—not from 9 p.m. to 11 p.m. as Jan had assumed. Jan tried to get to Chicago in time, but ended up missing the checkpoint. ∎

This filing system was constructed using Sealine chart holders designed for use while canoeing or kayaking. The system protects paperwork from the weather, yet provides easy access to several pages of information.

tion you're willing to travel during each leg of the rally, it's easy to discount these "sucker" bonuses.

When I participated in the 1995 Iron Butt Rally, I knew I would have 23 hours to travel from Salt Lake City to Spokane, Washington. The fastest route, using interstate highways, would have required riding about 720 miles and would have taken a little more than ten hours at legal speeds. I ran several scenarios and determined that I should go no farther east than Cheyenne, Wyoming. That would require about 20 hours of riding and would leave some time for rest and for other bonuses along the way. With this preplanning, it was easy to eliminate the first-leg sucker bonus in Anchorage, Alaska. I actually wound up capturing a bonus that was 130 miles beyond Cheyenne, but at least it was easy to see that it was in the proximity of my farthest possible calculation.

Whether you intend to navigate via GPS or with notes scribbled on index cards, it's important to mark all bonuses on regional maps. Bonuses with relatively low point values may not make it to your plotted route, but later in the rally, if you encounter unexpected road construction, severe weather, or other delays, you may have to forgo the bonuses you had originally chosen to capture some unplanned, lower value bonuses instead. It's easier to recognize these opportunities if they are marked on the map.

After marking your map, make an initial route by plugging bonuses into the skeleton routes you previously set up. It doesn't matter in what order you insert the bonuses into the skeleton. If you have Automap Pro, you'll use the optimize feature to determine the best order for collecting the bonuses. Don't worry about whether there will be sufficient time to collect all of them; there almost certainly won't be. Let the computer determine how many hours must be cut from the route for you to make it to the next checkpoint on time.

After your program has calculated a route of potential bonus stops, inspect it to see if you recognize logical candidates for elimination. Sometimes the program will display a route with rogue spurs that require you make a side trip to a bonus and backtrack to rejoin the main route. Unless unusually high points justify these "whiskers," drop them and plot the route again. If the revised route with the reduced bonuses still requires more riding time than you have, continue to eliminate bonuses until you have a plan that fits within the constraints of the rally.

Riding Your Plan

My procedure for keeping on schedule has changed since I began using a GPS receiver. Prior to GPS, when I was satisfied with my intended route, I would record the estimated arrival times for a half-dozen or so of the bonus stops on 3x5 cards. By referring to these cards, I could tell if I was making my key bonuses on schedule. If I fell seriously behind, I knew I would have to find a way to make up lost time or drop some planned bonuses.

Since adopting GPS, I no longer bother with 3x5 cards. The GPS unit will report my overall average speed for the leg, and I know how many hours remain to the next checkpoint. When you know the total mileage of a leg including bonus stops, you can easily calculate the average speed you must maintain to arrive at the checkpoint on time. If you see that your average speed is falling below the required speed, you must either make better time or drop some of the bonuses from your plan. If your average speed exceeds the required speed, you can either take additional time to rest or go for an additional bonus.

Some riders use countdown timers (and dual countdown timers) to tick off the time they have to reach the next checkpoint. On dual timers, the second clock is often used for timing pit stops. Many of the timers that I've seen have been purchased at Radio Shack.

Keeping notes. I'm not aware of anyone who uses a computer to print Roadbooks during a rally (see Chapter 3: Trip Planning and Organization). The process would be too cumbersome and time consuming, and you would need to have a printer as well as a laptop computer. But, I've seen a lot of endurance riders who use small models of the Touratech Roadbook device to manually write key instructions and information on a roll of Roadbook paper.

If you want to take notes while riding in foul weather, you can buy "Rite in the Rain" all-

Lisa Landry completed the 2001 Iron Butt Rally on her Harley-Davidson. She also served as a member of the rally staff, photographing the activities at the checkpoints.

Reading Comprehension 102

1999 Iron Butt winner George Barnes can also attest to the value of good reading comprehension, based on his 1997 Iron Butt Rally ride.

There was an especially huge bonus available to riders who rode to Springfield, Missouri. George plotted his route, headed for Springfield, and stopped to take a motel room for the evening shortly before his arrival.

When George awakened he reviewed the detailed instructions for collecting the bonus and realized he had plotted a route to the wrong Springfield. He was close to Springfield, Illinois—not Springfield, Missouri.

George paid a little closer attention to the bonus listings in the 1999 Iron Butt Rally—and won. ■

Gone With the Wind (Twice)

During the 1995 Iron Butt Rally, I neglected to close the zippers to my tankbag after making a pit stop in Texas. At some point between Abilene and Fort Worth, I lost the envelope that contained proof of the numerous bonus locations I'd visited since departing San Diego. I spent almost eight hours backtracking in a vain attempt to find the missing receipts. Although I lost hundreds of bonus points, I didn't lose my determination to continue the rally. I vowed not to let such a thing happen again.

One year later, I participated in the 8/48 Rally, in which competitors attempted to visit the 48 contiguous states in fewer than eight days. After visiting more than 40 states, I once again lost the receipts that validated my ride. At the banquet following the rally, I was ceremoniously given the Velcro Award for my "uncanny ability to snatch defeat from the jaws of victory by losing paperwork in two separate rallies." The rallymaster suggested that I should carry some Velcro with me so I could attach my receipts to the motorcycle.

I finally began hanging a passport wallet around my neck, under my shirt, to store gasoline receipts, photographs, and other important rally paperwork, and I haven't lost anything since. ■

This necklace passport wallet provides a convenient way to keep your receipts with you. Ensuring that you don't lose paperwork is an important consideration during endurance rallies.

George Barnes ultimately won, he nearly fell victim to such influence. George had planned to visit the Canyonlands National Park bonus location on his way to Texas. Another rider, whom he met along the way, convinced him there wasn't sufficient time to collect the bonus and still make it to Texas on time. George had changed his plan and decided to forgo the Canyonlands, when he stopped to carefully recheck his previous assumptions. After rebooting his laptop computer and repeating his calculations, he was convinced again that he could make the ride. He continued to the Canyonlands before riding to Texas and ultimately won the rally.

Unless something convinces you it's necessary to change your original plan, it's often best to stick with your chosen strategy rather than second-guess yourself in the middle of the road. Time spent questioning the wisdom of your intended route is usually unproductive and sub-

weather writing paper from J.L. Darling Corporation. The paper was created specifically for writing field notes in all-weather conditions—from the torrential downpours of the Pacific Northwest to the blistering heat and humidity of Florida. Your windshield can also be a convenient place for you to scribble quick routing notes or other important reminders with a grease pencil.

Mind games. Even veteran riders sometimes question their own judgement because of doubts expressed by fellow competitors. During the second leg of the 1999 Iron Butt Rally, which jects you to additional stress. So what if you haven't selected the optimal plan? As long as you ride responsibly and cautiously, a rally isn't a life-or-death matter.

Managing Paperwork

Endurance riders must deal with both instruction sheets and bonus listings distributed at the beginning of the rally, and documentation needed to substantiate bonus stops. Depending on the duration of the event, instructions and bonus listings can run a dozen pages or more in length, and since you will be referring to this info throughout a rally, it's important to have a method for keeping everything intact and dry.

Many riders attach a series of plastic notebook pages to the top of their tankbag into which they can insert maps, bonus listings, and other notes so they can refer to them without dismounting and digging through their luggage. Most of the notebooks I've seen were custom made specifically for the purpose.

The only commercial product I've seen that compares to these homemade solutions were assembled of waterproof zip-lock chart holders meant for use on sailboats and kayaks. D-rings at each corner of the chart holders allow you to put three or four of them together with twist-ties or other fasteners to create a booklet that you can attach to the top of your tankbag with small bungie cords.

Evidence of having visited a bonus might require an instant photograph; sometimes your motorcycle and rally towel must appear in the photograph and sometimes you must appear in the photograph (which makes a camera with a self-timer very useful). Other times you may need a printed receipt from a gas station or other specified location. Additional information, such as time of day and odometer reading, usually must be recorded on the instruction sheets or bonus listings.

No matter how you decide to manage your paperwork, it's critical that you develop a specific routine and stick with it. Some riders print a small checklist, have it laminated, and place it under the window of their tankbag or fasten it somewhere on the motorcycle where they can reference it after a pit stop or bonus stop.

Voice recorders. When collecting bonuses for the Utah 1088, you are sometimes required to answer a specific question from information you must locate at a certain roadside historical marker, gravesite, milepost, or other sign along the highway.

Endurance rider Gary Eagan always wears a small voice recorder under his riding suit attached to a cord around his neck. When he arrives at such bonus locations, he can quickly record his motorcycle's odometer reading as well as the information required to collect the

George Barnes

In 1999, George Barnes set a new mileage record for the Iron Butt Rally when he rode 13,346 miles during the 11-day event. In addition to this first-place finish, George has won numerous other endurance rallies, including the Cal 1+1, the Utah 1088, and the Thin Air TT Rally, which he won in 1999 and in 2000. He won the Thin Air TT Rally while riding two-up with his son.

George's father had been a motorcycle policeman with the Los Angeles Police Department. He taught George to ride a Cushman Trailmaster when he was only nine years old. While in his early 20s, George had a "dream job" with the west coast distributor of Moto Guzzi: putting 1,000 miles on brand new bikes so that the dealer could perform maintenance service before delivering them to the police department.

George won the Iron Butt Rally in 1999 after shedding 30 pounds and giving up caffeine during the two months prior to the rally. He also made it a point to swim for an hour or so each day before the event to temper the pre-rally excitement that otherwise kept him awake. ■

1. Select a pay-at-the-pump station and park so you won't have to walk around the motorcycle to lift it onto the centerstand.

2. Keep your credit card handy.

5. While you're filling the main tank, remove the cap from the auxiliary tank.

6. As you're filling the auxiliary tank, close the filler cap on the main tank.

bonus—often without dismounting. Gary then transcribes the necessary information onto the bonus sheets before turning them in.

Pit Stops

One of your best opportunities to improve your overall rally performance is to polish your pit stop routine. During the course of a long rally, such as the Iron Butt, you'll make between 50 and 80 stops for fuel, depending on your motor-cycle's fuel capacity and your ability to stay in the saddle. Chopping a minute or two from each stop can provide additional *hours* of riding time (or sleep) over the course of a rally.

Some riders argue that pit stops should be leisurely because they provide an important opportunity to get some much-needed relaxation and a break in your pace. I wouldn't discourage any rider from taking whatever time is needed to feel comfortable and safe, but the most successful en-

3. Put the card into the machine for authorization.

4. Move the tankbag and open the filler cap for the main fuel tank. If you normally reset your odometer after every fill-up, do it now.

7. Last step: collect the receipt and fill out any necessary paperwork.

8. With practice, you should be pulling away from the pump about five minutes after you arrive.

durance riders streamline their pit stops as much as they can.

After winning the 1999 Iron Butt Rally, George Barnes described his approach in an article for the BMWMOA. George treated the 11-day Iron Butt Rally as "11 consecutive Utah 1088s." The Utah 1088, which George has also won, is a 24-hour rally in which winning is dependent on efficient pit stops. During the Iron Butt, George tried to maintain the discipline needed to focus on short pit stops for the duration of the 11-day event.

George strives to keep his time at the pump to less than four minutes, including filling his main tank and the auxiliary tank. Typically, less than eight minutes will have elapsed from the time he leaves the highway to enter a filling station until he's back up to highway speed again.

Norm and Linda Babcock

Norm and Linda Babcock may well be the long-distance riding community's most heavily-traveled couple. In 1998, the year Norm and Linda were married (on Valentine's Day), for the first time in the history of the BMWMOA Mileage Contest, a man and wife individually won the men's and women's categories. Norm rode 46,318 miles and Linda rode 39,278 for the year. In 2000, Norm and Linda each finished in second place in their respective categories, another BMWMOA Mileage Contest first.

In addition to their mileage contest achievements, each of them has completed an IBA SaddleSore 1000, a Bun Burner, a Bun Burner Gold, and a 50CC. Norm has completed two Iron Butt Rallies, six Alberta 2000s, and numerous other endurance events. Linda has completed two Alberta 2000s and was an ardent competitor in the Team Strange "I've Been Everywhere Tour" and the Team Strange "President's Tour."

Norm and Linda are both Tour Leaders for Ayres Adventures. Linda leads tours in North America and helps administer the company's women's program. Norm specializes in leading tours through the National Park systems in the United States and Canada.

Norm has developed a routine for eating while riding that he believes has served him very well on many long trips. He packs several small baggies in his tankbag, each filled with four or five Fig Newtons. A butt pack with twin bottle holders is strapped to his tankbag so that he has a few bottles of Gatorade close at hand.

"I always wear a flip-up helmet," Norm says, "so whenever I feel a hunger pang I reach into the bag, slip out a Newton, and pop it into my mouth. If my mouth isn't already dry, it will be by the time I've swallowed the Newton, so I wash it down with a slug or two of Gatorade. I satisfy my hunger pang, ensure that I remain hydrated, and I'm not tempted to stop at the next fast-food restaurant." ■

Develop a Routine

Successful pit stop routines vary from one rider to the next, but most competitive riders share some tricks. First, try to use automated pay-at-the-pump stations, to avoid becoming hung up in a line at the cash register, and keep your credit card handy so you don't have to rummage through your wallet for it. If you need to put your bike on its centerstand to completely fill the fuel tank, pull up to the right of a pump so you can save yourself the time of walking around the bike to lift it onto the centerstand.

After dismounting, remove your gloves and insert your credit card into the reader for authorization while you are opening the lid to the fuel tank. If you're riding a motorcycle equipped with an auxiliary tank, you should have time to open the lid to both tanks before the authorization process is complete. If you use your tripmeter to keep track of the distance you've traveled since refueling, reset it now.

When the fuel tanks are full, replace the hose and push the buttons needed to request a receipt. Close the lid to the fuel tank and replace the tankbag while the receipt is printing. If you must visit the restroom, you can file your receipt away in your wallet while walking away from the pumps. During alternate stops, do a brief walk around the bike to inspect the tires for damage and proper inflation and check the engine oil level.

What *Not* to Do

To make pit stops as efficient as possible, what you *don't* do is just as important as what you do. Don't take time to clean the windshield at each pit stop. Except on large touring bikes, most riders look over the windshield—not through it. You'll suffer no loss of visibility by letting the windshield accumulate some dirt and bugs.

Clean the face shield of your helmet if it's so dirty that it annoys you, but don't take the time to clean it at every stop. If your windshield is adjusted properly, it should direct the wind stream at the top of your helmet rather than at the center of it. Most dirt and insects will be deflected from the face shield, making it unnecessary to clean it at every stop.

Finally, don't stand around eating or drinking while parked. It's more productive to do it while you're riding. If you're hungry, purchase a pre-packaged sandwich, open the cellophane wrapper, and place it in your tankbag before leaving the station.

Eating to Win

In observance of the dictum to do everything that you can on the motorcycle and to rely on maintaining a steady, consistent pace, serious competitors eat while moving. I sometimes pack energy bars and small packages of beef jerky to snack on while riding. Many riders pre-cut energy bars into small, bite-sized pieces and sprinkle them with powdered sugar to prevent their sticking together.

I'm very disciplined about the system that I follow when I'm competing in an endurance rally. Beginning in the morning, I eat nothing but fresh fruit and fruit juices. Bananas, oranges, peaches, nectarines, and plums are readily available and are easy to carry on the motorcycle. But I never eat fruit with, or immediately following anything else. Once I've eaten anything but fruit, I wait at least three hours before eating fruit again. If I eat flesh (meat or fish), I wait at least four hours. I drink a lot of water all day long and eat nothing after about eight o'clock in the evening.

I developed this routine after reading *Fit for Life,* by Harvey and Marilyn Diamond. What I found intriguing about their program is their claim that it frees up energy, since a prime objective of an endurance rider is to maximize the amount of vital energy at one's disposal. Their program is based not on *what* you eat, but *when* you eat it and in what combinations. I'm not an expert in the field of nutrition, but the program seems to work for me and is easy to follow during a demanding ride.

Theoretically, the digestion of food requires a great deal of energy, and some foods and food combinations require more energy to digest than others. Flesh, for instance, requires the most energy to digest, especially if eaten more than once per day. We're often sleepy after a large meal because so much energy is needed for digestion. When digestion consumes less energy, you will

Gagging on Jerky

Like many riders, Iron Butt competitor Bryce Ulrich often enjoys snacking on jerky while riding. During one ride on a dark, remote Pennsylvania highway at 70 miles per hour, Bryce crammed a large piece into his mouth. He suddenly realized that he wasn't able to swallow the mouthful, as it was "stringy" and wouldn't go down. After a few moments, he realized that he wasn't able to breathe. He executed a panic stop and pulled onto the shoulder, convinced he was within moments of blacking out.

Bryce was terrified as he began wheezing. Once he came to a stop, he began tugging at his helmet, when his gag reflex suddenly kicked in. His eyes were streaming tears and he was shaking all over as he choked the jerky out of his throat. He was so exhausted from the experience that he stopped early for the night.

Bryce still eats jerky while riding, but he recommends you buy packages with small pieces, or cut the longer strips down to size before taking off. ∎

have more in reserve for use elsewhere—like staying alert and concentrating on riding.

In *Fit for Life,* there's an "energy ladder" that recommends which foods should be consumed early in the day, and which should be consumed later:

AM
Fresh Fruit & Fruit Juices
Fresh Vegetable Juice and Salads
Steamed Vegetables, Raw Nuts & Seeds
Grains, Breads, Potatoes, Legumes
Meat, Chicken, Fish, Dairy
PM

Although I haven't found it practical to have salads and fresh fruit juice during an endurance ride, it's permissible to extend the consumption of fruit until later in the day. I usually continue to eat fruit until after lunch, then add some nuts and

The cockpit of Iron Butt competitor Jeff Earls's BMW R1150GS includes many practical goodies, including a Garmin III Plus receiver, Lynde-Ordway coin changer, Littlite map lamp, Valentine V1 remote radar readout (next to the GPS receiver), drinking tube (near the coin changer) and notes on the interior of the windshield.

Bill McAvan's ultra-clean Harley-Davidson cockpit showcases some of his custom work. The switches above the left handgrip control the passing lamps (which have been modified to long-range driving lights), fog lamps, map light, and cyclometer light. Behind the switches, Bill has installed a rheostat to control his electric vest. The platform holds a Garmin Street Pilot GPS receiver, a radio-controlled clock, and a Radio Shack dual timer. The right handlebar sports a Sigma BC-1100 bicycle cyclometer.

seeds from packages of trail mix that are available at convenience stores.

I typically eat flesh no more than once per day. A 20-minute stop at a Subway shop provides a roasted chicken, turkey breast, or tuna salad sub. If I'm pressed for time, I'll grab a prepackaged chicken salad or tuna salad sandwich from a convenience store instead and eat it while standing at the gasoline pump. Except for an occasional ice cream bar, I avoid dairy products.

Paying Tolls

When traveling in parts of the country where toll plazas are common, you'll need a convenient method of getting your hands on some coins without rummaging through your tankbag or removing your wallet from your riding suit. One inexpensive solution is to use Velcro to attach a small inexpensive coin holder to the outside of your tankbag, or to the motorcycle itself. You can find such items at virtually all stores that sell automotive accessories. Metal coin changers like those used by fast-food vendors and video arcade personnel are available from such companies as Lynde-Ordway and can be ordered in any configuration desired. JC Whitney also sells a small chrome coin holder with a handlebar mount.

Clothing and Laundry

For endurance rallies lasting a week or more, riders must pack enough clean clothing to see them through the event, since visiting a laundromat or submitting laundry to a hotel or motel laundry service won't be feasible. Some motorcyclists with limited luggage capacity will be challenged to carry sufficient changes of clothing.

Some riders mail packages of fresh clothing to checkpoints or hotels prior to the rally. Dirty clothing is discarded at checkpoints rather than packed and carried along. To minimize the trauma of throwing away clothes, they wear old items that they don't mind parting with. Some riders go so far as to purchase secondhand clothing prior to the rally.

Teaming Up

Whether to ride an endurance rally with another competitor or to ride it alone is a popular topic of conversation among endurance-riding enthusiasts. Although it's common to see two-up teams during a one-day or two-day rally, it's unusual for couples to make it through the 11-day Iron Butt Rally. In 1995, Ron and Karen McAteer became the first two-up couple to finish the Iron Butt on a Honda ST1100. In 1999, Archie and Irene Bailey finished on a Kawasaki Concours and Michael and Carolyn McDaniel spent their honeymoon riding two-up on their Ducati.

When it comes to individual competitors riding their own motorcycles, there are advantages and disadvantages to riding together, and the answer will ultimately come down to a matter of personal preference. In most circumstances, I believe I'm safer alone than teamed with another rider. It would be unusual for me to find another rider whose requirements for food and rest coincide exactly with mine. If I were traveling with a weaker rider, I would be annoyed by more frequent and potentially longer stops than I require and I would always be concerned about the comfort and safety of the other person. On the other hand, if I were teamed with a stronger rider, I would be tempted to continue to ride beyond the point at which I would otherwise have stopped to rest, as I'd be reluctant to slow him down.

I've considered riding rallies with another rider, and have sometimes teamed up with someone to travel to a specific bonus location before going my own way again. I often enjoy riding with friends whose style and temperament are similar to mine, but when running a competitive endurance rally, I prefer to go solo.

Riders who travel together have arguments to support their decision. One is the adage that two heads are better than one. They claim to avoid the trap of biting off more than they can chew. In addition, it's less tiring to follow an experienced rider than it is to blaze the trail alone, always in the lead position. In the unfortunate event of a mechanical breakdown or other mishap, the advantages of having a friend along are obvious.

Although there have been some instances in which two riders shared first place after riding together during a short rally, the big events have traditionally been won by solitary riders. Manny Sameiro and Harold Brooks are the most notable

Michael and Carolyn McDaniel

Michael and Carolyn McDaniel made history when they spent their honeymoon together, two-up, on their Ducati—participating in the 1999 Iron Butt Rally just two days after they were married. Before the wedding, the McDaniels discussed their guest list. "We'll have to find out how to invite all the folks from the long-distance community. They're the only people we really like," Carolyn had said. During the rally, they realized that they had serendipitously managed to do just that. Their friends and fellow Iron Butt competitors provided a rolling reception that circumnavigated the continental United States. They enjoyed the rally so much that they repeated the feat in 2001—again riding two-up on a Ducati.

Carolyn says she has been asked how they could accomplish such a ride without wanting to kill each other.

"I am surprised at the question," Carolyn said. "This sort of conflict doesn't come up for us because our goals are the same: we want to ride safely, have fun, and do our best. It helps that Michael and I are so similar in temperament and ability to endure, and that our biological rhythms seem to be in sync. We never have issues about one of us wanting to stop when the other one doesn't."

Michael and Carolyn are both registered nurses. To help soften their 11,000-mile, 11-day Iron Butt butts, they use the sort of gel pads that are normally placed under surgery patients on the seats of their motorcycle. ∎

Archie and Irene Bailey completed the 1999 Iron Butt Rally two-up on a Kawasaki Concours. Only a few couples have finished an Iron Butt Rally riding two-up.

duo to finish near the top of the Iron Butt Rally, riding together to tie for third place in 1999.

Insurance

Rallymasters require proof of insurance for entrants in their rallies, but there has always been some question as to whether a rider's insurance company would challenge a claim if a serious accident occurred during an endurance rally. Most policies exclude coverage for an accident that occurs during a competitive event.

To my knowledge, in every instance of an accident that occurred during a rally, the insurance company has honored the claim—although it's possible that no accident has been sensational enough, or involved a large enough liability claim, to attract their suspicion. It's also unlikely that the insurance companies were aware the mishaps occurred during a competitive event.

Rallymasters generally don't publicly identify competitors prior to a rally, supposedly in response to this eventuality. If that's the purpose of holding entrants' names confidential before a rally begins, it probably won't accomplish much. The names of riders are posted online once a rally starts, and accidents, as infrequent as they have been, are published on the Internet.

If you're planning to participate in an endurance rally, however, you should consider the possible implications to your insurance coverage.

When the Pavement Ends

This book has been about long-distance travel on paved roads. If you're happy to stick with the highways, perhaps your off-road riding will be limited to an occasional gravel parking lot or unpaved driveway. You can rack up tens of thousands of miles traveling back and forth across the United States and never leave the pavement. Even in construction zones, you usually won't encounter anything more challenging along interstate highways than making your way through temporary lanes divided by concrete barriers. Once you leave the Lower 48, however, things can change quickly.

If you're more adventuresome and you want to visit remote destinations, it will be helpful if you know the elementary rules about riding off the pavement. If you intend to seek out unpaved roads for *extended* trips or travel in less developed countries, you'll need more than basic pointers; you should do some additional reading and enroll in an off-road riding course.

Even if your *intentions* are to stay on paved highways, if you extend your riding to include Alaska or northern Canada, you may be surprised to see how often you encounter some rough going. Construction zones in Canada often extend for ten miles or more and frequently entail riding through dirt, gravel, and even mud. Things are even worse south of the border. It would be a pity to ruin a dream vacation because you don't know the basics about handing the rough stuff. It would also be a shame to refrain from making what could be the trip of a lifetime

Approaching the Bulembu border crossing in Swaziland during the rainy season: you never know how bad things may get when you leave the pavement.

Chris Scott

London-based adventure motorcyclist Chris Scott is one of the world's foremost authorities on travel in the Sahara. Since 1980 he has undertaken more than 20 expeditions across the Sahara and has visited every country except

(photo courtesy of Chris Scott)

Chad, which he plans to do in 2002. He has also traveled the desert regions of southern Africa, Australia, and North America.

Chris's first motorcycle adventure got him halfway to Wales aboard a moped at age 16. After 12 years of dispatch riding in London, Chris made several motorcycle journeys to the Sahara. The trips were described in *Desert Travels: Motorbike Journeys in the Sahara and West Africa.*

Today Chris maintains various travel guidebooks and web sites, including www.adventure-motorcycling.com, and produces travel videos. He frequently returns to the Sahara where he occasionally runs tours on either two or four wheels.

In his *Adventure Motorcycling Handbook,* Chris offers some very important advice to riders who are venturing off the pavement for the first time:

"Standing up on the footrests over rough ground is probably the most important technique off-road riding neophytes should master because when you're standing up:

- Suspension shocks are taken through your legs not your back
- Your bike is much easier to control
- Being higher up, your forward vision is improved

"Contrary to the impression that standing up raises your center of gravity and makes you less stable, it, in fact, has the opposite effect. It transfers your weight low, through the footrests, rather than through the saddle when you're seated. This is why trials riders and motocrossers always tackle tricky sections standing up on their pegs." ■

for fear that you won't be able to handle an occasional construction zone.

Several years ago, while participating in the Alberta 2000 Motorcycle Endurance Rally with about 60 experienced long-distance enthusiasts, we came upon a construction zone in British Columbia. The zone was more than five miles long and included several sections with deep mud. At least a dozen experienced "pavement pounders," including me, dropped our motorcycles as we slogged through the mud. My motorcycle was disabled after the valve cover was ripped open by rocks beneath the surface of the mud and I had to have it transported to the BMW dealer in Edmonton in the back of a pickup truck. That was one of the few times I had ever had my motorcycle off the pavement and it was the first time I had ever ridden through mud. If I had learned a few basic principles of riding off-pavement first, I probably would have avoided the mishaps. Although the construction zone was rugged, even by Canadian or Alaskan standards, it wasn't necessary to participate in an endurance rally to find it. If I had been touring British Columbia, which I've done frequently, I would have had to either negotiate that stretch or take a few-hundred-mile detour.

Keeping it Upright

Except that you'll have to allow more time to stop, riding on a well graded, hard packed dirt or gravel road isn't particularly challenging and doesn't require much more skill and experience than riding on pavement. Dual-sport motorcycles, large touring bikes, and even sport bikes can generally handle a stretch of smooth, hard-packed dirt or gravel. But what are the keys to staying upright when things beneath your tires become a bit sloppy?

First, until you gain some experience and confidence riding off-road, ride very cautiously. Traction is unpredictable in the dirt and if you become overconfident after riding through some tightly packed dirt, you may be taken by surprise when the surface changes. Chris Scott, in his highly acclaimed *Adventure Motorcycling Handbook,* advises that as a general rule you shouldn't exceed 50 mph on any dirt surface, as it's not possible to react quickly enough if the terrain changes quickly. I'd advise even slower speeds to someone who doesn't have off-road experience.

Scott also advises that standing up on the footpegs over rough ground is probably the most important technique off-road riding neophytes should master. While you may think the practice would raise your center of gravity and make the motorcycle less stable, the opposite is true. Standing transfers your weight to the footpegs, thus lowering your center of gravity and making it easier for you to control the bike. In addition, since you'll be higher and will be able to see a little farther, you should get some advance warning about obstacles that are coming up.

It's easier to stand on the footpegs of some motorcycles than others. As you stand, grip the tank gently between your legs to provide additional stability. Practice this technique at slow speeds when there isn't any traffic, so you will be comfortable with it when you need it.

In his off-road training program, Paris-Dakar competitor Jimmy Lewis emphasizes a second important tip: loosen up on the controls—don't grasp the handlebars in a death grip when the going gets tough. "A moving motorcycle will tend to stay upright by itself," Jimmy advises. "You won't accomplish anything productive by gripping the controls tightly. Stay relaxed."

It's also generally a good idea to use a midrange gear when you are riding on unpaved surfaces. By keeping the motorcycle's rpms a little higher, you can use the braking power of the engine to slow down, rather than relying on the brakes, which is more likely to result in a skid. The additional torque available at the higher rpms will also help if you have to increase your speed briefly to make it through a rough stretch.

In addition to staying loose on the controls, standing on the pegs, and gearing down a bit, here are a few pointers you may find helpful for dealing with the most common off-pavement conditions:

• Dirt—Keep your speed down to provide additional time to stop, even if the road seems level and hard-packed. Don't permit yourself to be lulled into a false sense of security.

Jimmy Lewis is one of the world's top dirt riders, and he operates a school for off-road riding in the United States. Jimmy is pictured in Africa during the 2000 Paris-Dakar Rally. (courtesy of Jimmy Lewis)

On loose footing, you are more likely to stay upright if you relax your grip on the handlebars.

- Sand—If you encounter a short patch of sand, keep moving and open the throttle a little to shift some weight to the rear of the motorcycle to prevent the front wheel from digging in. The technique should get you through a short patch. Riding through extended areas of sand, or very deep sand, is

The author (right) and Tony Black at the Arctic Circle in Alaska. This sign is surely the most photographed site along the Dalton Highway.

Travel on gravel roads in Alaska can present an entirely new set of hazards. The scene adds new meaning to the term "meals on wheels."

another matter, as you obviously can't accelerate forever. Desert riding techniques are beyond the scope of this book, but are discussed in depth in Scott's *Adventure Motorcycling Handbook.* The techniques are also included in the curriculum of most off-road training programs.

If you're inexperienced and you encounter *deep* sand in a construction zone, your best alternative is probably to slow down and paddle through (sitting on the bike with your feet on the ground) at less than a snail's pace until you're out of it. Stay off the front brake and let the sand slow you down.

- Gravel—Shallow patches of gravel usually aren't difficult to deal with, but if the gravel is deep, the technique will be similar to riding in sand. Keep moving, and open the throttle a little to shift weight to the rear of the bike. The problem with deep gravel is that deep ruts are often formed by the passage of heavy four-wheeled vehicles. Avoid crossing the berms on each side of the rut. If you must cross them, do it slowly and as perpendicular to the berm as possible. If necessary, paddle through them.

- Mud—If you encounter a muddy patch (as opposed to deep mud) pick one muddy rut and stay with it. If you're comfortable standing up, try to make it through that way, slow and easy, without making abrupt changes to the accelerator or brakes. If you're not confident tackling it this way, paddle through it at a walking pace.

Handling slick, muddy surface conditions is challenge enough. What's worse is that as mud fills the treads of your tires, traction will deteriorate even more. That's one reason knobby tires are favored for extended off-highway riding; unless they are subjected to *deep* mud, knobbies are less likely to become clogged and lose their traction.

During the years after my misadventure in the British Columbian mud, I acquired some off-highway experience. I rode my K1100LT (the same BMW touring motorcycle that I had dropped in the Alberta 2000 five years and a few hundred thousand miles earlier) more than 6,000 miles through British Columbia, the Yukon, and Alaska. In addition to long stretches of dirt and gravel on the Alaska Highway, the Klondike Highway, and the Cassier Highway, I rode the gravel Dalton Highway from Fairbanks to the Arctic Circle. Except for losing my driving lights to flying stones and a tire puncture, I made the trip without incident and had a great time, a feat I attribute, at least in part, to my following the practices recommended above.

These tips won't make you an expert off-road rider, but if you observe the pointers and take it easy until you gain additional training and experience, you'll find it a lot easier to stay upright as you negotiate the occasional bad patch.

Taking It Off-Road

So much for dealing with the occasional bad patch of road, but why would anyone intentionally leave the paved world behind? First, there's an "off-pavement" world out there that many experienced long-distance riders are hardly aware of. After all, there are many more miles of unpaved roads in the world than there are paved ones, and this is especially appealing to adventuresome riders who enjoy camping and want to get closer to nature. But you'll trade one set of risks for another. Traffic may be so light that you can all but forget about motorists making left turns across your path, drivers distracted during cell phone conversations, or vehicles unexpectedly entering the road from parking lots or side streets. In exchange for this, you must expect poor (and unpredictable) road conditions and a greater likelihood of falling down. Most of these new risks can be mitigated if you exercise caution and get some additional training.

If you're going to pursue long-distance riding off-highway, there are several things you should consider before venturing off the beaten path.

Touring vs. Dual-Sport Motorcycles

Depending on the amount of off-highway riding you plan to do, and the difficulty of the terrain you want to tackle, you'll probably soon learn the significant advantages offered by lightweight dual-sport motorcycles. Although an experienced rider exercising caution can enjoy many of the continent's unpaved roads on a standard

Ramey "Coach" Peticolas-Stroud

Coach and his wife Cynthia own a 60-acre ranch in the Cascade Mountains of Oregon. The ranch includes a bed and breakfast that's decorated in a motorcycle motif and a stable with a collection of dirt bikes and dual-sport motorcycles. Here, at the headquarters of the Cascade Endurance Center, Coach provides training for professional racers and factory drivers and riders. The school also offers basic off-road motorcycle training.

The winner of the Best in the Desert off-road racing championships in 1999 and 2000, Coach is an expert motorcyclist and roadracer. He's completed the longest off-road race in American history, riding solo in a three-person team event. He's competed in superbike events at Willow Springs International Raceway, Formula USA, WERA, and Portland International Raceway. Winning numerous classes, he finished 15th overall in OMRRA as a private rider against factory and professional racers. He finished third overall in the California Championship Cup Series "Super Singles," an unlimited expert competition.

Coach is also an accomplished international motorcycle traveler. He's ridden from the Arctic Circle to Panama, throughout Central America, and in North Africa.

Coach has some advice for novice off-road riders: "Realize that a death grip on the handlebars will wear you down. Fear of losing control is often the cause. When you grab the handlebars, you compress the nerves in your hands and wrists. Eventually the nerves will become irritated and your hands will tingle, then go to sleep. You must learn to improve your riding skills enough to develop a relaxed riding style."

The BMW GS has many fans among adventure-touring riders and is quite at home in moderate dirt conditions. For extended going on very rough terrain, however, BMW's lighter weight F650 would have the advantage. (photo by Daniel Cohen)

Getting to this spot near The Valley of the Gods in southeastern Utah requires riding on some gravel.

motorcycle, touring motorcycles, sport bikes, and cruisers aren't generally suitable for extended off-highway travel. Forget what you've heard about Iron Butt Rally competitors successfully making it up and down the famous "haul road" between Fairbanks, Alaska, and Prudhoe Bay on touring bikes. The riders were some of the most experienced in the world, and most of the touring bikes were severely trashed by the beating they were given.

The suspension systems on touring motorcycles aren't designed to handle the rigors of off-highway travel. Even after setting a motorcycle's pre-load to the maximum setting, the motorcycle will bottom out more quickly than a dual-sport motorcycle or a dirt bike, especially if you've packed it with camping gear and are riding two-up. The rims of touring bikes also can bend easily and using a maximum pre-load setting can increase the likelihood of damaging your wheels.

In addition, many touring motorcycles are liquid-cooled and the radiators aren't designed to withstand extremely dirty or muddy conditions. Even when flying rocks and debris don't do damage outright, radiators tend to become clogged, which can lead to overheating, especially at the lower speeds one typically uses off-road.

The fairing and body components of touring motorcycles aren't designed to handle off-highway conditions either. There typically isn't much clearance between the fenders and the wheels, and this space can become packed with mud, which not only can cause the fenders to break, but also contribute to severely deteriorated handling. Unlike touring and sport bikes, dual-sport and dirt bikes are also usually designed to withstand being dropped without disabling the motorcycle or entailing costly repair bills for broken components like luggage cases, mirrors, and turn signals.

Pre-Load Settings and GVWR

The importance of observing GVWR (Gross Vehicle Weight Restrictions) was discussed in Chapter 3: Trip Planning and Organization. Not exceeding a bike's maximum carrying capacity is important for touring on paved highways, but it's even more critical if you're going off-highway. In addition to the increased stopping distance needed on dirt or gravel, and the importance of an unimpaired suspension system, there is a greater likelihood of falling down while riding off-highway. An overloaded motorcycle not only increases the risk of a fall, but you'll have a much more difficult time getting an overloaded motorcycle upright again.

Rest More Frequently

Just as off-highway riding places additional stress on your motorcycle, it will also place more stress on you. The cumulative effect of the bumps and vibrations that you'll encounter will cause you to tire more quickly than if you're cruising along a paved highway. The additional diligence and concentration needed while riding off-highway will also tire you. Be prepared to stop more frequently for rest.

Even if you prefer to not wear a kidney belt while touring on the highway, you may find it helpful for improving comfort and reducing fatigue when your body is subjected to the additional stress of riding off-road. Besides, if you have the misfortune of dropping your motorcycle, a good kidney belt may prevent your injuring yourself as you're struggling to get the motorcycle upright.

Riding the Corrugations

Although riding on dirt is a lot easier than dealing with gravel, rocks, and especially mud, there's plenty that can go wrong very quickly on a dirt road: ruts, areas covered over by blowing sand, and stretches that have been washed away by the rain, exposing rocks and creating more ruts. What can be even worse are the corrugations found on some dirt roads, especially those subjected to travel by heavy vehicles. Those are the times when you'll really appreciate a nice, tight kidney belt.

Accelerating up to about 50 mph will allow you to skim across the top of each ripple, which can significantly reduce vibration. Since your wheels will barely be touching the ground, your traction will be reduced significantly. While this is risky even on a straight stretch, it's treacherous on a bend, as you're likely to skid off the road. If you're going to try skimming, keep a watchful

Helge Pedersen

Norwegian motorcyclist Helge Pedersen is one of the world's best-known professional touring motorcyclists and is familiar to the world's motorcycle press. In his epic book, *Ten Years on Two Wheels,* Helge captured photographs during his quarter-million-mile odyssey through 77 countries. He is one of only a few motorcyclists to have traveled through the infamous 80-mile-long Darien Gap, and the only one to have done it from Colombia to Panama.

In addition to sharing his epic travels via photography, Helge also leads small groups of motorcyclists in around-the-world tours. Additional information on Helge's tours can be found at his web site: www.globeriders.com ∎

(photo courtesy of Helge Pedersen)

eye out for bends in the road and slow down before entering them.

On many corrugated patches, you'll find the ripples to be much shallower near either edge of the road. It's often possible to get a smoother ride by staying at the extreme edge of the track. In some cases, the ripples are much worse in one lane than they are in the other, as when you're climbing or descending a steep grade. One of my favorite rides is the unpaved road leading up to

Utah Route 261 in the Valley of the Gods in southeastern Utah. Portions of the track are badly corrugated, but it always seems smoother when I ride in the left lane while making the climb, as the corrugations seem less severe on the downhill lane. Obviously, it's important to be on the lookout for oncoming traffic so you have plenty of time to move back into your own lane.

Buddy-Up

With the prevalence of cell phone service and the ability to flag down traffic, travel on most North American highways is relatively safe. It's often a different story when you venture off the pavement. There are many deserted roads in North America where cell phones don't work and it can be hours, or even days, before seeing other traffic.

Ride with a friend when you head off the paved highways. The chances of a mishap increase and the chances of quickly finding needed help decrease. When traveling in remote areas, it's beneficial to have someone along who can help you if you encounter difficulty.

Be Prepared for Punctures

Carry a tire repair kit and inflation device and know how to repair your own punctures. The likelihood of having a puncture increases dramatically depending on both tread wear and the amount of riding that's done on unpaved surfaces. New tires with a lot of tread are much less susceptible to punctures than are tires that have had most of the tread worn away.

Don't Drive at Night

Even when driving at reduced speeds, it's very dangerous to ride off-highway after dark. You won't have lane markings and fog lines to help you identify where the road is going and in the dark it will be much more difficult to read changes in the terrain. Also, depending on where you're riding, you may face the additional danger of animals on the road at night. If you have an

This lone rider is taking in some spectacular scenery in Monument Valley, Utah.

accident on an unpaved road after dark, it may be a long time before someone comes along to help you.

Time your trips so you'll be sitting around a campfire or checked into your hotel or lodge before the sun goes down.

Protect the Lights

For riders who travel extensively on unpaved roads, the addition of an inexpensive headlight shield is necessary to avoid the inconvenience and cost of losing a headlight. It can be unbelievably expensive to replace a cracked or rock-chipped headlight lens.

Riderwearhouse offers the StonGard Headlight Shield, a cut-to-fit, thick flexible vinyl film that can be affixed to the headlight of virtually any model of motorcycle. Other types of headlight shields are available from a variety of off-highway motorcycle accessory suppliers.

Use Sturdy Luggage Cases

Traveling off-highway, and presumably camping rather than staying in motels, makes the selection of luggage cases even more important than with trips that are restricted to the pavement. Adventurous world travelers often eschew stock luggage cases in favor of aluminum panniers. Many stock luggage cases have a capacity of less than 50 liters; aluminum pannier systems typically hold twice that amount. The aluminum systems are also much sturdier. BMW plastic cases are notorious for falling off the motorcycle during hard, off-highway riding. I've personally lost both BMW plastic panniers and a top case while touring off-highway. Leading suppliers of aluminum pannier systems include Jesse, Touratech, Hepco & Becker, Bernd Tesch, and Happy Trails.

Expand Your Checklist

For adventure motorcycling, it's wise to augment your checklist. At the minimum, you should carry more food and water than you would otherwise. Depending on how far from civilization you expect to be, consider bringing an emergency blanket and a means of making a fire. If you aren't camping and already packing a tent, a tarp can come in handy. In an emergency,

Camping in the great outdoors is enjoyable and can significantly reduce your travel costs.

at least two ends of a tarp can be secured to the motorcycle to provide a makeshift lean-to shelter.

For extended riding in deep sand or mud, it's helpful to reduce tire pressure. If you plan to do this, you'll also have to pack a portable compressor or air pump to inflate them again when you're finished with the soft stuff.

Finally, if there's a chance you'll have to count on a passing truck to haul your motorcycle back to civilization, take along some tie-downs.

Get Some Training

If you intend to travel off-road extensively consider getting some off-highway motorcycle training. World-class racer Jimmy Lewis holds off-road classes, usually in California or Nevada, for beginners as well as for experienced riders. Ramey "Coach" Stroud offers training courses at his Cascade Endurance Center in Lyons, Oregon. With either of these schools, you can either use your own motorcycle or you can rent a lightweight dirt bike from the school.

Check with the Motorcycle Safety Foundation too. Although they apparently don't offer courses in all parts of the country, their web site lists a dirt-bike school under their training programs.

If you intend to travel extensively off-pavement, consider getting some specialized training in off-road riding techniques. (photo by Daniel Cohen)

If you can't make it to one of these programs, check with your local motorcycle dealer, as dirt-bike schools are often offered locally through clubs or by dealers who carry a line of dirt bikes. If your local dealer doesn't offer such a training program, they can often refer you to a course in your area.

Additional Reading

If you're interested in the subject of adventure travel, there are several books on the topic. One of the best books on the subject of riding off-highway is *The Adventure Motorcycling Handbook,* by Chris Scott. Chris's book includes tips on selecting an appropriate off-highway motorcycle, preparing the motorcycle for adventure touring, and tips about riding in a variety of conditions.

World adventurer Dr. Gregory Frazier has also written several books about touring remote areas of the world, including *BMW GSing Around the World.* He's also written articles for *Motorcycle Consumer News* on equipping a motorcycle for an around-the-world trip.

Whether you're a veteran camper or you're new to the topic of motorcycle camping, you'll find Bob Woofter's book, *Motorcycle Camping Made Easy,* an important addition to your library. Bob's book covers virtually every aspect of camping from a motorcycle, from outfitting yourself to mastering the skills necessary to have a good time.

Perhaps one of the motorcycling community's best-known world travelers is Norwegian Helge Pedersen, the author of *Ten Years on Two Wheels.* His book isn't about the technical aspects of off-road riding, but it will provide an interesting glimpse into what it's like to spend ten years traveling around the world by motorcycle.

CHAPTER 7

Resource Directory

Lists of sources for motorcycle accessories become outdated or obsolete quickly, especially for suppliers of specialized equipment of interest to the long-distance community. Many are small companies, or even individual entrepreneurs, who enter and leave the market frequently. Most small companies have a web site. Use a good search engine, such as Google, to locate suppliers of specialized equipment.

If you have difficulty locating any equipment or services, try subscribing to the LDRider Internet list. The list isn't brand-specific and placing an inquiry to members of the long-distance community will usually elicit the information required. You can also subscribe to one of the brand-specific Internet chat lists, such as the Internet BMW Riders list. Most typically maintain easy-to-access archives with information regarding the motorcycles of interest to their membership. H. Marc Lewis maintains a web site dedicated to motorcycling, and Carl Paukstis maintains an extensive list directory, the Mailing List Roundup, on Marc's web site.

Of course, the Iron Butt Association is the foremost organization dedicated to the sport of long-distance touring, and their web site contains a wealth of information on long-distance events.

Other Reading

Keep a copy of David L. Hough's book, *Proficient Motorcycling,* at your bedside and refer to it often. It's the best book I've found on improving riding skills. I also recommend another of David's books, *Street Strategies,* for improving your survival tactics in traffic.

Read U.S. Air Force Survival Instructor, Gregory J. Davenport's book, *Wilderness Survival,* for a discussion of the theory of dressing properly for harsh weather conditions. The book is also interesting reading for anyone who would like to know how to set a snare, tan an animal's hide, or distinguish edible wild plants from poisonous ones.

Products and Services

Products and Services			
Company	**Description**	**Web site/E-mail address**	**Phone/Fax**
Apparel			
ActionStations, Inc.	Distributors of Bohn body protection products for motorcyclists, and such accessories as CoolMax undergarments	www.actionstation.com	(888) 922-9269 (530) 898-9188 (fax)
Adventure Motorcycle Gear	Rukka Clothing—vented riding suits for riding in hot weather	www.adventuremotogear.com	(800) 217-3526 (703) 913-7261 (fax)
Aerostich Riderwear and Riderwearhouse Catalog	Wide variety of clothing and accessories for the motorcycle enthusiast	www.aerostich.com	(800) 222-1994 (218) 722-1927 (218) 720-3610 (fax)
Altberg Ltd.	U.K. based manufacturer of motorcycle boots—they ship to the U.S.	www.altberg.co.uk	
Chilli Heated Clothing, Ltd.	Heated waistcoats, Schuberth Helmets, and other accessories	ds.dial.pipex.com/chilli Chilli@calamander.co.uk	
DuPont CoolMax	Read about CoolMax, which is incorporated into some motorcycling garments	www.dupont.com/coolmax	(800) 342-3774
Gerbing's Heated Clothing	Electrically heated clothing	www.gerbing.com	(800) 646-5916 (360) 898-4223 (fax)
Intersport Fashions West, Inc.	First Gear riding clothing and Schuberth helmets	www.intersportfashions.com	(800) 416-8255 (714) 258-7511 (fax)
Joe Rocket	Motorcycle riding gear, including Phoenix jacket and pants for hot weather riding	www.joerocket.com	(800) 635-6103 (208) 523-7390 (fax)
LDComfort	Seamless underwear	www.ldcomfort.com	(800) 634-4874 (877) 648-0955 (fax)
Marsee	Cooling vest for hot weather riding, hydration systems, and other riding gear	www.marseeproducts.com	(800) 293-2400 (909) 600-9441 (fax)
Motoport	Weatherproof motorcycle clothing and accessories, including Tri-Armor	www.motoport.com	(800) 777-6499 (760) 233-7561 (fax)
Olympia Sports	Manufacturer of a wide line of motorcycle gloves	www.olympiagloves.com	(800) 645-6124 (914) 347-4737 (914) 347-2029 (fax)
Red Wing Shoe Company, Inc.	Rugged outdoor and occupational footwear	www.redwing.com	(800) 733-9464 (800) 733-9464
Ride Cool	MiraCool vest—cool vest for hot weather riding	www.ridecool.com	(817) 488-4504
Rocky Shoes and Boots	Rugged outdoor and occupational footwear	www.rockyboots.com	
Sidi Sport	Italian manufacturer of motorcycle boots and other sportswear	www.sidisport.com	
SmartWool	Wool socks and other warm-weather gear	www.smartwool.com	(800) 550-WOOL
Spidi Sport Wear	Complete line of motorcycle clothing directed at the sport riding market, including "flow through" clothing for hot weather riding	www.lockhartphillipsusa.com/spidiintro.html	
Thorlo, Inc.	Athletic socks (backpacker and hiker) for motorcycling	www.thorlo.com	(800) 457-2256 (704) 838-6323 (fax)
Tourmaster	Jackets and one-piece suits	www.tourmaster.com	(800) 455-2552
Ultra Cool/Gioello Enterprises Ltd.	Ribbed ventilating undergarments for use in hot weather	www.rvuultracool.com	(914) 963-4837 (914) 965-0852 (fax)

Products and Services			
Company	**Description**	**Web site/E-mail address**	**Phone/Fax**
Vanson Leathers	Leather motorcycle clothing, including a full line of perforated leathers for warm weather use	www.vansonleathers.com	(508) 678-2000 (508) 677-6773 (fax)
Viberg Boot Manufacturing Ltd.	Several models of motorcycle boots, made to measure with custom features available	www.workboot.com	(800) 663-6388 (250) 361-9372 (fax)
Warm & Safe Inc.	"Heat Troller" thermostat for heated clothing	www.warmnsafe.com	
Z Custom Leathers	Manufacturer of custom leather suits, gloves, boots, jackets, and pants	www.zcustom.com	(714) 890-5721 (714) 890-5723 (fax)
Audio & Communications			
Air Rider	Motorcycle audio—radios and headsets	www.airrider.com	(888) 232-9253 (800) 251-6040 (800) 777-5240 (423) 238-5387 (fax)
Autocom	Motorcycle audio—radios and headsets	topgear@worldnet.att.net	(888) 851-GEAR
Cycle Com	Radio systems	www.cyclecomm.com	(800) 251-6040 (423) 238-5387 (fax)
E&E Products	"Tank Tunes"—sound systems in a tankbag	www.tanktunes.com	(888) 575-8980 (386) 676-0164 (fax)
J&M Corporation	Motorcycle audio—radios and headsets	www.jmcorp.com	(800) 358-0881 (520) 624-7000 (520) 624-6202 (fax)
Kennedy Technology Group, Inc.	CellSet, RadarSet, and CBSet for connecting cellular phone, radar detector, and CB into motorcycle helmet headsets	www.cellset.com	(316) 776-1111
Now Hear This	Custom made earplugs, including earplugs with integrated speakers (Marilyn Navia, M.S., CCC/A)	plugup@aol.com	(305) 477-2333
Versabag	Manufacturer of tankbag stereo systems	my.dmci.net/~watkinsrd/menu.htm	(888) 770-1010 (517) 437-4416 (fax)
Ear Plugs			
Lab Safety Supply, Inc.	Wide assortment of disposable and reusable earplugs	www.labsafety.com	(800) 356-0783 (800) 543-9910
Now Hear This	Custom made earplugs, including earplugs with integrated speakers (Marilyn Navia, M.S., CCC/A)	plugup@aol.com	(305) 477-2333
The Earplug Company	Custom fit hearing protection for motorcyclists	www.earplugco.com	(407) 895-6216
Fuel Tanks & Supplies			
Brown Motor Works, Inc.	Auxiliary fuel tanks, auxiliary lighting	www.brownbmw.com	(909) 629-2132 (909) 397-5145 (fax)
Champion Sidecars	Tour Tank auxiliary fuel tank for saddlebag installation in Honda Gold Wing	www.championsidecars.com	(800) 875-0949 (714) 847-1539 (fax)
Fuel Safe Racing Cells	Auxiliary fuel cells	www.fuelsafe.com/index.html	(800) 433-6524 (541) 388-0203 (541) 388-0307 (fax)
Jaz Products	Auxiliary fuel systems	www.jazproducts.com	(800) 525-8133

| \multicolumn{4}{c}{**Products and Services**} |
Company	**Description**	**Web site/E-mail address**	**Phone/Fax**
Sampson Sporttouring Products	Auxiliary fuel systems, Hyper-Lites, handlebar risers, highway pegs, and more	www.sampson-sporttouring.com	
Smith, Ron	Auxiliary fuel systems and light brackets for Gold Wings	www.eztank2.com	(425) 481-8536 (425) 402-9173
Summit Racing	Performance parts and equipment, including Summit Fuel Cells (auxiliary fuel tanks)	www.summitracing.com	(800) 230-3030
GPS Units & Accessories			
Garmin Corporation	Navigation and communication equipment (GPS). User manuals for Garmin GPS receivers can be downloaded from this web site	www.garmin.com	
GPS City	Full line of GPS receivers and accessories	www.gpscity.com	(800) 231-7540 (866) GPS-CITY (702) 990-5603 (fax)
James Associates	Internet supplier of GPS receivers and software, including software for the Mac	www.macgpspro.com	(303) 258-0576 (303) 258-0373 (fax)
REI	Sealine waterproof map cases, Therm-a-Rest sport seats, GPS receivers, and software	www.rei.com	(800) 426-4840 (253) 891-2523 (fax)
Saeng	Cockpit mounts for radar detectors and GPS units, and Quick-Scan wide-angle mirrors	www.saeng.com	(800) 868-7464 (402) 562-6777 (fax)
Helmets			
Helmet City	Source for most popular brands of motorcycle helmets	www.helmetcity.com	(888) 343-5638
Heated Grips			
Hot Grips Mfg., Inc.	Manufacturer of heated handgrips for most makes of motorcycle	www.hotgrips.com	(603) 448-0303 (603) 448-0305 (fax)
Intersport Fashions West, Inc.	First Gear riding clothing and Schuberth helmets	www.intersportfashions.com	(800) 416-8255 (714) 258-7511 (fax)
Schuberth Helmets	Schuberth helmets	www.schuberth.de	
Shoei	Shoei motorcycle helmets	www.shoei.com	(714) 730-0941 (714) 730-0942 (fax)
Information, Organizations & People			
American Automobile Association	Roadside Assistance Programs	www.aaa.com	
American Motorcyclist Association	Protects and promotes the interests of motorcycle enthusiasts	www.ama-cycle.org	(614) 856-1900 (614) 856-1920 (fax)
Barr, Dave	Motorcycle adventurer, author and inspirational speaker	www.davebarr.com	(888) 213-2503
Bernd Tesch	German motorcycle world traveler and manufacturer of motorcycle travel equipment	www.berndtesch.de/English/EIndex.html berndtesch@gmx.de	
BMW Motorcycle Owners of America	Club for owners of BMW motorcycles—sponsor of BMW Annual Mileage Contest	www.bmwmoa.org	(636) 394-7277 (636) 391-1811 (fax)
Cohen, Daniel	National Parks Tour	www.danielcohen.org	

Products and Services			
Company	Description	Web site/E-mail address	Phone/Fax
Deming BBQ	Annual motorcyclist gathering, especially members of the long-distance community	www.nmpcs.com/Deming/	
Frazier, Dr. Gregory W.	Professional motorcycle adventurer—source for books on global travel, including off-highway travel	www.horizonsunlimited.com/ gregfrazier	
Gold Wing Road Riders Association	Club for owners of Gold Wing (and other) motorcycles. Roadside Assistance Programs, Gold Book Program	www.gwrra.org	
Harley Owners Group	Club for owners of Harley-Davidson motorcycles. Roadside assistance programs	www.hog.com	
Honda Rider's Club of America	Club for owners of Honda motorcycles—Roadside Assistance Programs	www.hondamotorcycle.com/ hrca	
Horizons Unlimited	Resource information for the motorcycle world traveler	www.horizonsunlimited.com	
Hyder Seek	Annual dinner in Hyder, Alaska, in recognition of 49-state IBA Rides	www.ronayres.com	
Internet BMW Riders	BMW motorcycling club and mailing list with resource information about BMW motorcycles	www.ibmwr.org	
Iron Butt Association	"The Source" for endurance riding information	www.ironbutt.com	
LDRiders	Mail list for riders interested in long-distance riding	www.ldriders.com	
Lewis, H. Marc	Mailing list services and a directory of motorcycling-related Internet mailing lists	www.micapeak.com	
Long Distance Pieces and Parts	A directory of sources for parts, supplies, and services of interest to the long-distance community	webmaster10.com/ldr/ index.html	
Long Distance Riders' Help List	A voluntary list of long-distance riders who have agreed to help other riders with emergency assistance or with certification of long-distance rides	home.earthlink.net/ ~webmaster10/ld/ldr-form.htm	
Mailing List Roundup	Provides a compilation of motorcycle-related mailing lists available via Internet electronic mail	www.micapeak.com/ mailinglistroundup	
MERA (Motorcycle Endurance Riders Association)	MERA web site enables motorcyclists to find information about endurance rallies, and to recognize personal records for both time and distance. The site also has information about the Utah 1088 Rally	www.utah1088.com	
Pedersen, Helge	Author, tour leader for international tours, gives seminars on international touring	www.globeriders.com helge@globeriders.com	
Sanders, Nick	Accomplished world traveler who leads groups of motorcyclists on around-the-world trips	www.nicksanders.com	
Southern California Motorcycle Association	Sponsors of the Four Corners Tour and the Three Flags Classic Motorcycle Rally	www.sc-ma.com	
STOC (Honda ST Owner's Club)	Club and mailing list for owners of the Honda ST series of motorcycles	www.st-riders.com	

Products and Services			
Company	**Description**	**Web site/E-mail address**	**Phone/Fax**
United Sidecar Association	An independent organization of enthusiasts who own motorcycles with sidecars attached	www.sidecar.com	
United States Department of Transportation	The Federal Highway Administration maintains a web site of America's Scenic Byways Program, providing a directory of some of the most interesting highways in the nation	www.byways.org	
United States National Park Service	The National Park Service maintains a web site with a directory and information about National Parks and National Monuments	www.nps.gov	
Whitehorse Press	Books, videos, and accessories for motorcycle enthusiasts	www.whitehorsepress.com	(800) 531-1133 (603) 356-6556 (603) 356-6590 (fax)
Lights & Accessories			
Baja Designs	HID lighting systems and off-road accessories	www.bajadesigns.com/index.html	(800) 422-5292 (760) 560-0383 (fax)
Brown Motor Works, Inc.	Auxiliary fuel tanks, auxiliary lighting	www.brownbmw.com	(909) 629-2132 (909) 397-5145 (fax)
Hella, Inc.	Auxiliary lighting systems	www.hellausa.com	
Kisan Technologies	Manufacturer of Tire Alert pressure monitoring device, taillight modulators, and headlight modulators	www.kisantech.com	(719) 226-0300 (719) 576-4700 (fax)
Littlite/CAE, Inc.	Gooseneck lamps for illuminating tankbag maps and instruments	www.caeinc.com	(810) 231-9373 (810) 231-1631 (fax)
Martin Fabrication	Light mounts and GPS mounts for BMW motorcycles	www.martinfabrication.bigstep.com	
Motolight	Additional halogen lighting	www.motolight.com	(800) 567-8346 (513) 474-7731 (fax)
P.U.M.A.	Auxiliary lighting systems	www.puma-access.com	(800) 354-3552 (800) 333-7862 (440) 498-9647 (fax)
Philips	Auxiliary lighting systems	www.lighting.philips.com	
PIAA	Auxiliary lighting systems, including HID driving lights	www.piaa.com	
Sampson Sporttouring Products	Auxiliary fuel systems, Hyper-Lites, handlebar risers, highway pegs, and more	www.sampson-sporttouring.com	
Smith, Ron	Auxiliary fuel systems and light brackets for Gold Wings	www.eztank2.com	(425) 481-8536 (425) 402-9173
Luggage & Tank Bags			
Custom Tank Bags by Linda Tanner	Custom tankbags, fuel cell covers, and motorcycle luggage	www.customtankbags.com	(866) 304-2138
Givi Motorcycle Accessories	Removable hard-sided luggage systems, soft-sided luggage, helmets, windscreens, and other accessories	www.givi.it	
Happy Trails Motorcycle Products	Luggage systems and equipment for off-highway use	www.happy-trail.com	(800) 444-8770 (208) 377-8772 (fax)

Products and Services

Company	Description	Web site/E-mail address	Phone/Fax
Helen TwoWheels	Helen TwoWheels' Super Packing System—everything you need to know about properly packing a motorcycle	www.helen2wheels.com	(734) 662-2008 (734) 662-4843 (fax)
Hepco & Becker	Off-highway motorcycle luggage and accessories	www.hepco-becker.de	
RKA	Motorcycle luggage and apparel, including CoolMax shirts	www.rka-luggage.com	(800) 349-1752 (707) 433-3743 (fax)
Touratech	German manufacturer of motorcycle accessories for off-highway "adventure touring" and rally computers and accessories, including the Roadbook. Also provides aluminum luggage systems designed for off-highway use	www.touratech-usa.com	(800) 491-2926 (206) 323-2349 (206) 325-6016 (fax)
Versabag	Manufacturer of tankbag stereo systems	my.dmci.net/~watkinsrd/menu.htm	(888) 770-1010 (517) 437-4416 (fax)

Maps & Map Software

Company	Description	Web site/E-mail address	Phone/Fax
ALK Technologies, Inc.	TravRoute software to support PC-based GPS functions and handheld and pocket PC devices—best-suited for in-vehicle use	www.travroute.com	(888) 872-8768 (609) 252-8197 (609) 252-8108 (fax)
Cascade Designs, Inc.	Sealine transparent map cases, Therm-a-Rest mattresses, and Sport Seats	www.cascadedesigns.com	(800) 531-9531 (800) 583-7583 (fax)
DeLorme	Distributors of Street Atlas USA mapping software, the Atlas and Gazetteer series of detailed regional street atlases, and Earthmate GPS receivers	www.delorme.com	(800) 511-2459 (800) 575-2244 (fax)
REI	Sealine waterproof map cases, Therm-a-Rest sport seats, GPS receivers, and software	www.rei.com	(800) 426-4840 (253) 891-2523 (fax)

Miscellaneous Long-Distance Accessories

Company	Description	Web site/E-mail address	Phone/Fax
A&S BMW Motorcycles	Accessories include angle valve stems, AirHawk cushions, handheld air compressors, driving lights, and throttle locks	www.ascycles.com	(800) 689-9893 (916) 726-3563 (fax)
Aerostich Riderwear and Riderwearhouse Catalog	Wide variety of clothing and accessories for the motorcycle enthusiast	www.aerostich.com	(800) 222-1994 (218) 722-1927 (218) 720-3610 (fax)
Bob's BMW	BMW parts and accessories, including luggage "bag liners" for virtually all models of BMW, and for the Wrist Rest Throttle Lock	www.bmwbobs.com	(800) BMWBOBS (301) 497-8949 (301) 776-2338 (fax)
CBT Imports	Distributor of many top lines of interest to the long-distance community, including PIAA, Staintune, and Top of the Line	www.cbtimports.com/index.html	(800) 782-4686 (650) 938-9663 (fax)
Cycle Gadgets	Accessories of interest to long-distance riders, including GPS receivers, cockpit mounts, and the infamous Screaming Meanie	www.cyclegadgets.com/default.htm info@CycleGadgets.com	(877) 7GADGET (877) 742-3438) (530) 348-7485 (fax)
CycoActive, Inc.	U.S. distributor for Touratech luggage systems, GPS systems, and many other motorcycling accessories	www.cycoactive.com	(800) 491-2926 (206) 323-2349 (206) 325-6016 (fax)
Dennis Kirk	Parts, tires, helmets, exhaust, apparel, and accessories	www.denniskirk.com	(800) 328-9280 (320) 358-4019 (fax)

Products and Services

Company	Description	Web site/E-mail address	Phone/Fax
J. L. Darling Corporation	Manufacturers of all-weather writing paper that permits you to write notes in the rain	www.riteintherain.com	(253) 922-5000 (253) 922-5300 (fax)
JC Whitney, Inc.	Automotive and motorcycle parts and accessories, including handlebar-mount chrome coin holder	www.jcwhitney.com	(800) 529-4486 (800) 537-2700 (fax)
Precision Manufacturing and Sales	Motorcycling tools and equipment, including the Coats and Corghi brands of tire changing and balancing equipment	www.precisionmfgsales.com	(800) 237-5947 (727) 446-1163 (fax)
Sampson Sporttouring Products	Auxiliary fuel systems, Hyper-Lites, handlebar risers, highway pegs, and more	www.sampson-sporttouring.com	
Stephenson's Warmlite	Mail order supplier of tents, sleeping bags, and rain suits, including "Vapor Barrier" clothing as an alternative to Gore-Tex	www.warmlite.com	
Touratech	German manufacturer of motorcycle accessories for off-highway "adventure touring" and rally computers and accessories, including the Roadbook. Also provides aluminum luggage systems designed for off-highway use	www.touratech-usa.com	(800) 491-2926 (206) 323-2349 (206) 325-6016 (fax)
Whitehorse Press	Books, videos, and accessories for motorcycle enthusiasts	www.whitehorsepress.com	(800) 531-1133 (603) 356-6556 (603) 356-6590 (fax)

Mounts & Holders

Company	Description	Web site/E-mail address	Phone/Fax
BLM Accessories	Custom-made shelves, mounts, and auxiliary fuel systems	www.blm-accessories.com	(425) 485-2065
Lynde-Ordway Company Inc.	Belt coin changers for paying tolls	www.lynde-ordway.com	(800) 762-7057 (714) 433-2166 (fax)
Saeng	Cockpit mounts for radar detectors and GPS units, and Quick-Scan wide-angle mirrors	www.saeng.com	(800) 868-7464 (402) 562-6777 (fax)

Off-Road Accessories

Company	Description	Web site/E-mail address	Phone/Fax
Adventure Rider	Resource information for the off-highway rider	www.advrider.com	
Baja Designs	HID lighting systems and off-road accessories	www.bajadesigns.com/index.html	(800) 422-5292 (760) 560-0383 (fax)
BestRest Products, LLC.	Provides a variety of accessories designed for dual-sport motorcycles, including a miniature air compressor, back rests, and cargo racks	www.bestrestproducts.com	(425) 673-1023 (425) 673-0502 (fax)
Cascade Endurance Center	Off-road training programs and motorcycle endurance training	www.ridecoach.com	(503) 580-0000
Jimmy Lewis Racing	Off-road riding schools	www.jimmylewisracing.com	
Touratech	German manufacturer of motorcycle accessories for off-highway "adventure touring" and rally computers and accessories, including the Roadbook. Also provides aluminum luggage systems designed for off-highway use	www.touratech-usa.com	(800) 491-2926 (206) 323-2349 (206) 325-6016 (fax)

Products and Services			
Company	**Description**	**Web site/E-mail address**	**Phone/Fax**
Pavement Wetting Systems			
E-Z Leaker	E-Z LEAKER is a device for those who wish to enjoy the call of the road without those annoying interruptions for the call of nature	www.ezleaker.com	(888) 704-0033
Liberated Spectator	Producers of "Stadium Pal"—a device to help riders avoid frequent pit stops	www.stadiumpal.com	(877) 782-3675
Radar Detectors			
Escort, Inc.	Escort radar detectors	www.escortradar.com	(800) 433-3487 (513) 942-8849 (fax)
Legal Speeding	Modifications for radar detectors for use on motorcycles	www.legalspeeding.com	
SJL Products	Radar protection products designed specifically for use on motorcycles, including Radar Screamer speaker and radar unit mounts	www.motorcycleradar.com	(508) 829-3339 (508) 829-3339 (fax)
Valentine	The Valentine One radar detector	www.valentine1.com	(800) 331-3030
Shock Absorbing Products			
Action Products, Inc.	Designer and manufacturer of pressure-relieving and shock-absorbing products for medical, sports, and specialty markets (AKTON pads for use on motorcycle seats)	www.actionproducts.com	(800) 228-7763 (877) 733-2073 (fax)
Safety Gear			
Galls	Public safety equipment and apparel—source for reflective tape	www.galls.com	(800) 477-7766 (800) 944-2557 (fax)
Hindsight	Provider of pre-cut reflective material for the back of BMW luggage	www.hind-sight.net	(801) 550-0438 (801) 760-4724 (fax)
JFF Enterprises	First-aid kits	www.hhjm.com/jff/jff.htm	
Motorcycle Safety Foundation	Motorcycle training programs	www.msf-usa.org	(877) 288-7093
Seats			
Bill Mayer Saddles	Custom-made motorcycle seats	www.billmayersaddles.com	(800) 242-7625 (805) 640-9147 (fax)
Cascade Designs, Inc.	Sealine transparent map cases, Therm-a-Rest mattresses, and Sport Seats	www.cascadedesigns.com	(800) 531-9531 (800) 583-7583 (fax)
Corbin Seats	Motorcycle seats, boots, and other accessories	www.corbin.com	(800) 538-7035 (800) 223-4332 (831) 634-1059 (fax)
Diamond Custom Seats	Custom motorcycle seats, primarily for large, touring motorcycles	www.diamondseats.com	(800) 722-9995 (386) 698-2762 (fax)
Hartco International	Motorcycle seats	www.hartcoseats.com	(386) 698-4668 (386) 698-2762 (fax)
Harwood Industries, Inc.	Racing and performance products, including auxiliary fuel tanks	www.eharwood.com	(800) 822-3392
Hopeland Custom Mfg., LLC	"Butt Buffer" polymer seat cushions	www.buttbuffer.com	(866) 859-5699 (717) 859-5699 (717) 733-9653 (fax)

Products and Services			
Company	**Description**	**Web site/E-mail address**	**Phone/Fax**
Mustang Motorcycle Seats	Custom seats	www.mustangseats.com	(800) 243-1392 (800) 243-1399 (fax)
Rick Mayer Cycle	Custom made touring and sport-touring motorcycle seats	www.rickmayercycle.com	(530) 357-2888 (530) 357-2888 (fax)
ROHO, Inc.	AirHawk seat cushion	www.rohoinc.com	(800) 851-3449 (888) 551-3449 (fax)
Russell Cycle Products, Inc.	Day-Long touring saddles	www.day-long.com	(800) 432-9566
Saddlemen Seats	Travelcade seats with gel inserts	www.saddlemen.com	(310) 638-1222 (310) 761-1234 (fax)
Sargent Cycle Products North America	Custom seats, tank accessories, seat covers, and leather cleaning products	www.sargentcycle.com	(800) 749-7328 (904) 355-5404 (fax)
Shipping			
Motorcycle Express	Shipping uncrated motorcycles internationally	www.motorcycleexpress.com	(516) 682-9220 (800) 245-8726 (516) 682-8231 (fax)
Tires & Accessories			
Avon Motorcycle Tires	Avon Tire information center, including fitment guide	www.coopertire.com/avon_motorcycle	(800) 624-7470 (425) 771-4246 (fax)
Dunlop	Dunlop Tire information center, including fitment guide	www.dunlopmotorcycle.com	
Inovex Industries, Inc.	Ride-On tire protection system—Tire sealant designed to prevent most tire punctures	www.ride-on.com	(888) 374-3366 (703) 421-1967
Metzeler Motorcycle Tyres	Metzeler motorcycle tire information center, including fitment guide	www.metzelermoto.com	
PerformanceBike	An internet marketing site for performance bicycles, but a source for the Airman handheld air pump	www.performancebike.com	(919) 933-9113 (800) 727-3291 (fax)
Stop & Go International Inc.	The Stop & Go Tire Plugger—tubeless tire repair kit	www.stopngo.com	(800) 747-0238 (815) 455-9080 (815) 455-9210 (fax)
Throttle Locks			
Schneider's, Inc.	Flip-A-Lever throttle locks	www.schneidersinc.com	(406) 822-4811
Timers & Rally Computers			
Radio Shack	One source for timers (and dual timers) used during endurance rallies	www.radioshack.com	
Sigma Sport	Cyclometers that are designed for bicycle use, but which have been adapted successfully for motorcycle use	www.sigmasport.com	
Touratech	German manufacturer of motorcycle accessories for off-highway "adventure touring" and rally computers and accessories, including the Roadbook. Also provides aluminum luggage systems designed for off-highway use	www.touratech-usa.com	(800) 491-2926 (206) 323-2349 (206) 325-6016 (fax)

Products and Services

Company	Description	Web site/E-mail address	Phone/Fax
Training			
Cascade Endurance Center	Off-road training programs and motorcycle endurance training	www.ridecoach.com	(503) 580-0000
Jimmy Lewis Racing	Off-road riding schools	www.jimmylewisracing.com	
Lean Bodies	Cliff Sheats's web site—information on Cliff's nutrition and fat loss program	www.leanbodies.com	(800) 697-5326
Motorcycle Safety Foundation	Motorcycle training programs	www.msf-usa.org	(877) 288-7093
Windshields			
Aeroflow	Windshields	www.aeroflowscreens.com	(888) 237-6777 (714) 777-4844 (714) 777-4682 (fax)
Givi Motorcycle Accessories	Removable hard-sided luggage systems, soft-sided luggage, helmets, windscreens, and other accessories	www.givi.it	
Gustafsson Plastics	Aftermarket windscreens	www.bikescreen.com	(888) 824-3443 (904) 824-2119 (904) 471-4897 (fax)
Parabellum, Ltd.	Windshields	www.parabellum.com	(706) 864-8051 (706) 864-5770 (fax)
Rifle Windshields	Motorcycle windshields	www.rifle.com	(800) 262-1237 (805) 466-9543 (fax)

Research Studies

Organization	Description	Web Site
Stanford University Sleep Center	Relationship Between Awareness of Sleepiness and Ability to Predict Sleep Onset	www.aaafoundation.org/resources/index.cfm?button=asleep
Federal Highway Administration	Commercial Motor Vehicle Driver Fatigue and Alertness Study	www.tc.gc.ca/tdc/publicat/tp12876/english/12876_e.htm
United States Navy	Performance Maintenance During Continuous Flight Operations—A Guide for Flight Surgeons (NAVMED P-6410, 1 January 2000)	
University of California at San Diego	Study for the Veterans Affairs Healthcare System on the brain's compensation for adverse effects caused by lack of sleep	health.ucsd.edu/news/2000_02_09_Sleep.html
Walter Reed Army Institute of Research	Studies about sleep-deprived soldiers in combat situations	www.usafa.af.mil/jscope/JSCOPE97/Belenky97/Belenky97.htm

More Touring Books From Whitehorse Press, the motorcycle information company

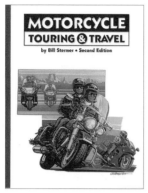

Softbound
8¼ x 10½ inches
160 pages
b/w/c illus.

Order Code: STER
Price: $19.95
ISBN: 1-884313-15-9

Motorcycle Touring and Travel: A Handbook of Travel by Motorcycle, Second Edition
by Bill Stermer

The book is a handbook for those interested in long-distance or long-duration travel by motorcycle. The author covers all important topics pertinent to planning and executing a trip by motorcycle: selecting the proper motorcycle and equipment, packing the right gear for a trip, dressing properly for various weather conditions, accommodating co-riders and other motorcyclists, camping, safety—and just plain having fun.

Softbound
8¼ x 10½ inches
176 pages
color illus.

Order Code: MCX
Price: $24.95
ISBN: 1-884313-01-9

Motorcycling Excellence: Skills, Knowledge, and Strategies for Riding Right
by The Motorcycle Safety Foundation

This book is the culmination of the Motorcycle Safety Foundation's 25-year development of safe riding strategies—including tips to help put yourself in the right frame of mind to ride, dress properly for safety and comfort, fix and identify small annoyances before they become big problems, spot traffic hazards and avoid them, travel skillfully in a group, steer quickly to avoid hazards, stop more quickly, pick your bike up, handle a trail bike off-road, and much more.

Motorcycle Journeys Through the Southwest
by Marty Berke   Order Code MJSW $19.95

Motorcycle Journeys Through New England
by Marty Berke   Order Code BERK $19.95

Motorcycle Journeys Through the Appalachians
by Dale Coyner   Order Code COYN $19.95

Motorcycle Journeys Through California
by Clement Salvadori   Order Code MJCA $24.95

Motorcycle Journeys Through the Alps & Corsica
by John Hermann   Order Code HERM3 $24.95

Motorcycle Journeys Through Southern Mexico
by Neal Davis   Order Code MJSM $19.95

Motorcycle Journeys Through Northern Mexico
by Neal Davis   Order Code MJNM $19.95

Motorcycle Journeys Through Baja
by Clement Salvadori   Order Code SALV $19.95

Get your free copy of the Whitehorse Press Motorcycling Catalog, featuring thousands of books, videos, tools & accessories.
Phone: 800-531-1133 or 603-356-6556; Fax: 603-356-6590
www.WhitehorsePress.com; Email: CustomerService@WhitehorsePress.com

Index

Other Titles by RON AYRES

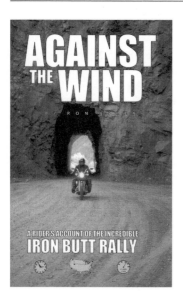

Against the Wind: A Rider's Account of the Incredible Iron Butt Rally
by Ron Ayres

Ten consecutive thousand-mile days on two wheels in a mental race against imponderable odds and a ceaselessly ticking clock— welcome to the legendary Iron Butt Rally. *Against the Wind* is a riveting book, written by sixth-place 1995 finisher Ron Ayres, telling the story of what many call the most grueling test of human endurance in all of motorcycling. With guts and shear willpower, riders must overcome (or succumb to) fatigue and danger, calling upon human reserves buried deep within. Ayres reveals the innermost thoughts of a successful contestant and lets us share the anticipation, the thrill, the fatigue, the heartbreak, the euphoria, and ultimately the controversy of completing this merciless trial. More than the mere mechanics of making it through the eleven-day ordeal, Ayres describes the elegant strategy necessary to be a contender. You'll discover what motivates the riders, how the rally is scored, what takes place each day, how the routes are planned, and what it's like to ride to the very limit of endurance—and then ride some more.

Softbound, 5 ½ x 8 ½ inches,
237 pages, 40 b/w illustrations
Order Code: AYRE
Price: $19.95
ISBN: 1-884313-09-4

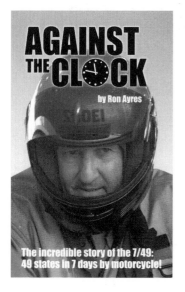

Against the Clock: The Incredible Story of the 7/49
by Ron Ayres

Did you love *Against the Wind*? We did. So we couldn't resist when Ron Ayres offered to write a book about shattering the Guinness Record for visiting the 48 contiguous states in 6 days and 31 minutes, then setting a new record by adding Alaska in exactly 7 days and 20 minutes after starting in Kittery, Maine on June 7th, 1998.

Against the Clock is the story of Ayres' historic ride, demonstrating the importance of teamwork in achieving a difficult objective many thought to be unattainable. It thoroughly captures the flavor of the ride as it happened: the internet community's reactions to the daily, hourly, even minute-by-minute updates, the frantic and chaotic e-mails concerning his condition, his mishaps, his personal and public victories, and finally, Ron's personal observations about his condition and concern for others. Displaying the trials and tribulations of the superhuman ride for the world to see with total sincerity, Ron shows why he has become a symbol of all that's good in the motorcycling community, and why he deserves the title "hero."

Softbound, 5 ½ x 8 ½ inches,
256 pages, b/w illustrations
Order Code: CLOCK
Price: $19.95
ISBN: 1-884313-19-1

Get your free copy of the Whitehorse Press Motorcycling Catalog, featuring thousands of books, videos, tools & accessories.
Phone: 800-531-1133 or 603-356-6556; Fax: 603-356-6590
www.WhitehorsePress.com; Email: CustomerService@WhitehorsePress.com

About the Author

Ron Ayres purchased his first motorcycle, a new Harley-Davidson Low Rider, in 1987 when he was 43 years old. To compensate for his late start, he began taking long trips on the motorcycle and was soon riding more than 500 miles per day. In 1995 he participated in his first motorcycle endurance competition, the Iron Butt Rally, and finished in sixth place. Ron was so fascinated with the rally, in which riders travel 1,000 miles per day or more for 11 consecutive days, that he felt compelled to write a book about it. More than the story of Ron's Iron Butt ride, *Against the Wind* is an engaging saga about the exhilaration and heartbreak experienced by the competitors of this incredible event. The book has become a Whitehorse Press bestseller.

The Iron Butt intensified Ron's appetite for endurance events and led to his participation in other rallies, including the Utah 1088 and the Alberta 2000. In 1998, he broke the existing Guinness record for riding a motorcycle through the 48 contiguous states. After completing the ride in a little more than six days, he continued to Hyder, Alaska, and established a new Iron Butt Association record category by riding to all 49 North American states in just seven days. Ron's second book, *Against the Clock,* recounts the story of this historic ride.

For Ron, it was always challenging to find time for riding and writing while a senior business executive with a global information technology company. But his business career provided an opportunity to live and work in Europe, South America, and Africa. In addition, he has had senior management responsibilities in Asia, Australia, the Middle East, and North America. His career provided the means for him to explore the world by motorcycle.

While Chief Executive Officer of EDS Africa, Ron was responsible for the company's business in sub-Saharan Africa. Living in Johannesburg, he and his wife Barbara purchased a Land Rover Defender, outfitted it for extended

(photo by Barbara Robinson)

travel in the bush, and took self-guided safaris through Botswana, Namibia, South Africa, and Zimbabwe. Ron retired from EDS in 1999 but remained in South Africa for several months to do additional safaris and to host an African motorcycle trip for a dozen Iron Butt veterans. He has continued to ride extensively and now enjoys riding off-road and camping by motorcycle. Although he still likes Harley-Davidson motorcycles, he found BMW touring bikes to be more suitable for endurance riding. More recently, he has gravitated toward BMW dual-sport machines.

Ron sponsors Hyder Seek, an annual gathering of riding enthusiasts. Each year, many long-distance devotees endeavor to earn the coveted Iron Butt "48 States Plus Alaska" award by culminating their own 49-state ride at a Hyder Seek celebration.

Ron's most recent business venture is Ayres Adventures, a global motorcycle touring company. In conjunction with his team of global tour leaders, he organizes and leads motorcyclists on trips through Africa, North America, South America, and other exciting motorcycling destinations.

Ron and Barbara live in Plano, Texas. When they aren't touring the world, they enjoy spending time with their three grandchildren.

Information about Ayres Adventures and Hyder Seek can be found on Ron's web site at www.ayresadventures.com.